LADY KILLERS

LADY KILLERS

Copyright © Octopus Publishing Group Limited, 2025

All rights reserved.

Text by Peter Salmon

No part of this book may be reproduced by any means, nor transmitted, nor translated into a machine language, without the written permission of the publishers.

Condition of Sale
This book is sold subject to the condition that it shall not, by way of trade or otherwise, be lent, resold, hired out or otherwise circulated in any form of binding or cover other than that in which it is published and without a similar condition including this condition being imposed on the subsequent purchaser.

An Hachette UK Company
www.hachette.co.uk

Summersdale Publishers
Part of Octopus Publishing Group Limited
Carmelite House
50 Victoria Embankment
LONDON
EC4Y 0DZ
UK

This FSC® label means that materials used for the product have been responsibly sourced

www.summersdale.com

The authorized representative in the EEA is Hachette Ireland, 8 Castlecourt Centre, Dublin 15, D15 XTP3, Ireland (email: info@hbgi.ie)

Printed and bound by Clays Ltd, Suffolk, NR35 1ED

ISBN: 978-1-83799-497-7

Substantial discounts on bulk quantities of Summersdale books are available to corporations, professional associations and other organizations. For details contact general enquiries: telephone: +44 (0) 1243 771107 or email: enquiries@summersdale.com.

LADY KILLERS

Shocking True Stories of the World's Most Barbaric Female Murderers

JAMIE KING

DISCLAIMER

All the stories in the book have been at some point expressed in the public domain. Every effort has been made to ensure that all information is correct. Should there be any errors, we apologize and shall be pleased to make the appropriate amendments in any future editions.

CONTENTS

Introduction   9

Crimes of Passion   15

Fatal Ambitions   89

Dark Secrets   151

Revenge and Retribution   211

Femmes Fatales   261

Final Word   315

INTRODUCTION

"The female of the species is more deadly than the male." – Rudyard Kipling

Of some species this is undoubtedly true – think of bees, hornets and wasps. It is only the female that carries a sting. Or the praying mantis, where the female consumes the male after intercourse, to provide protein for her eggs during gestation. Or the female golden eagle, so much heavier and more lethal than the male. And as is well known, it is only the female mosquito that draws blood and spreads malaria, the disease that kills millions of humans worldwide each year.

And then there is the black widow spider – so noxious is the female that a certain strain of female human murderers, those who kill their spouses, are called Black Widows. The male black widow is smaller and not deadly, but the female can deliver a bite with a venom 15 times stronger than a rattlesnake's. Solitary for most of the year, they find a male to mate with, and then, like the praying mantis, kill him and eat him, after turning him to liquid first.

But humans? Statistically, the male is far more violent – and yet... There are hundreds of people featured in this book who would have begged to differ: men, women and children who have met their end at the hands of the female of the species.

And not just the hands. They have been stabbed, shot, poisoned, drowned. Axes have come down on their heads, limbs have been removed, heads boiled and served up as food. They have been buried in shallow graves, turned into biscuits and soap, and carried about in trunks. If these dead could speak, would they not say the female of the species are the ones you really need to watch out for?

Some of the women in these pages killed just once; some of them killed again and again. Some gunned down schoolchildren, some drowned babies, some killed the elderly and ate them. For every Rosemary West or Myra Hindley, who seem to have plumbed the depths of brutality, there is a Belle Gunness or Tamara Samsonova, who give them a run for their money.

Take Russia's Irina Gaidamachuk – her vice was vodka, not murder, but how does one afford vodka if your husband won't give you money to buy any? For her the answer was simple: you find old women living alone and bludgeon them to death with an axe. So what if you're no good at saving? There's always another lonely woman to drop in on. Gaidamachuk didn't manage to kill as many as her eighteenth-century countrywoman Darya Nikolayevna Saltykova, who slaughtered 138 people in a mere six years, but who knows, if she had not been caught, Gaidamachuk might have added plenty more to her 17 victims.

And all Styllou Christofi wanted was for her son not to have married *that* woman. Doesn't a mother have the right to intervene? In her case, she intervened by hitting her on the head with a frying pan and then burning the body. Compared to the last time she committed a murder, when she'd shoved burning wood down the throat of her victim, one might say

INTRODUCTION

her daughter-in-law got off lightly.

Or what about Olga Hepnarová? Her plan was to kill as many people as possible, so she chose to drive a van into a crowded tram stop in her native Prague. She was disappointed to find only eight dead, especially as she had circled the tram stop for an hour beforehand, until there were enough potential victims gathered. She had sentenced society to death, she said, and soon after, society sentenced her to the same.

But not every killer in these pages is regarded as a villain. Some, like the biblical heroine Judith, are held in great honour, while others were driven to their crimes by abuse or humiliation. Some, like Charlotte Corday, who murdered the French revolutionary Jean-Paul Marat in his bath, are seen as heroes to some, but villains to others.

The female murderer can inspire as wide a range of feelings as the male. Some of these women's stories will have you cheering for them, and some will have you sighing with relief when they are caught and put away. Some you might mourn on the gallows or at the guillotine, some you might think got what they deserved. In these pages is all of life.

It can be hard to unpack what type of murder or murderer we are dealing with – is this a crime of passion, committed on the spur of the moment? Or was it premeditated, meticulously planned? Was the motive revenge or retribution, or did it simply come from the urge for financial gain? And was it a dark secret, or did the murderer act in plain sight?

In this book, the killings are divided into different chapters and different types, but don't forget, as you read each story, that any murderer acts for complicated reasons. One person's avenging angel is another's femme fatale.

LADY KILLERS

So put down that vodka, leave your biscuits to one side – who knows what is in them? – and join us on a journey into some of the darkest recesses of the human heart. But maybe lock the doors first...

And the next time you see a spider or a mosquito, treat her with respect. Because no matter how harmless they may look, who knows what deadly thoughts they harbour, and who knows when they will decide to strike? As someone once said, it is in their nature.

CRIMES OF PASSION

In some ways any murder is a crime of passion – completely passionless killings might be the stuff of films, but in real life it is rare for a murder to be committed without any emotion.

But in law, a "crime of passion" is one that is not premeditated – no planning happened, the murder just took place in that moment. It is usually subject to lighter sentences than a premeditated murder and is called second degree rather than first. This is why many defence counsels try to argue that a murder was spontaneous, and why evidence of planning can be devastating to the perpetrator.

There have been times – in France in the early twentieth century for example, as we will see in the case of Henriette Caillaux – where any murder by a woman was deemed a crime of passion. Women, according to this logic, were nothing if not creatures of passion. Could a woman really plan a murder? Being such delicate creatures, wouldn't they tremble even at the mere idea of taking a life? Wouldn't the knife drop from their hands as they fainted at the prospect? To actually kill, they must be enraged to a point where their feminine delicacy is overcome, if only for a moment.

The stories in this book give the lie to that assessment. Murders are planned, carried out and repeated by women in the same way as by men. We live, one might say, in more enlightened times.

But in this chapter, the line between a crime of passion and a premeditated murder is sometimes blurry. If being charged with second-degree murder is being given the "benefit" of the doubt, then this benefit is seldom all that great. And for the victim, it doesn't matter if their life was taken on the spur of the moment or after meticulous planning – the grave is just as cold.

In some of these cases, the passion is not just for the kill, but for the partner in crime. Many of the women featured here argued that they were manipulated into carrying out these heinous acts, and many of them were, no doubt, sincere in this. The threat of sexual and physical violence against them hangs over many of these stories, but it is often considered a tenuous defence and fails to convince. Judge them yourself as you will, but the law has already made its decision.

So, come on a journey where Rosemary West waits around one corner, and the Manson family around another. There will be guns, there will be knives, there will be pills. And of course, there will be blood, and lots of it.

HENRIETTE CAILLAUX – L'AFFAIRE CAILLAUX

It would become known as *L'Affaire Caillaux* – "The Caillaux Affair" – and it would captivate the entire French nation. It was a scandal that had everything – power, politics, sex, money and, of course, the most vital ingredient: murder.

And not just any murder – the murder of the editor of the biggest newspaper in France, then and now, *Le Figaro*. And not just any murderer – the murderer was the wife of a former prime minister who at the time of the killing was the finance minister. Not even the greatest of the French writers could have devised a plot so thrilling.

Late in the evening of 16 March 1914, Gaston Calmette, chief editor of *Le Figaro*, had just finished putting the following morning's newspaper to bed. An "elegant and sophisticated" woman strode into the building and along the corridor towards his office. She demanded to see Calmette, and was ushered in by an office worker, Adrien Cirac, who then closed the door. She was, after all, well known to all at *Le Figaro*, being the wife of Joseph Caillaux, the aforementioned finance minister.

A few brief words were exchanged. There was a pause. A few more words. And then six shots rang out. Cirac rushed back into the office to find Henriette Caillaux standing in front of the bookcase. In her hand she was holding a Browning pistol. At her feet, dead, was Gaston Calmette.

For years, Calmette had carried out a campaign against Joseph Caillaux, especially during his time as France's prime minister from 1911 to 1912, and again now that he was in charge of the country's finances. *Le Figaro* had printed letters which they claimed showed that Caillaux had been dishonest about several pieces of legislation. But it was Caillaux's personal life that Calmette had begun to attack – three days before Henriette visited his office, Calmette had printed an intimate letter that Caillaux had sent 13 years earlier to a mistress, and later wife, Berthe Gueydan. The letter showed he had been having an affair and also revealed suspect political dealings.

Henriette believed that her husband's reputation needed defending – but for the finance minister to challenge the editor of a newspaper to a duel was inconceivable. She was also worried that other intimate letters might appear – particularly those between herself and her husband.

For although the pair had been married in 1911 – becoming one of the richest couples in France – they had been lovers since 1907, despite both having been married to other people. Henriette, born Henriette Raynouard on 5 December 1874, had been married at 19 to a writer 12 years her senior, with whom she had two children. Joseph Caillaux, for his part, was known for his *liaisons élégantes* – "elegant connections" – and both Berthe Gueydan and Henriette had left husbands to be with him. Divorce had only been legalized in France in 1884, and Caillaux took full advantage of the new law. But in getting together, the pair had no doubt engaged in some romantic chicanery, which they would prefer not to appear in the press.

On shooting Calmette, Henriette was immediately arrested, and provided good copy for the newspapers, explaining to the arresting officer that as there was no more justice in France, she had resolved that she alone would be able to stop the campaign. She refused to be transported to the police headquarters in a police van, insisting on being driven there by her chauffeur in her own car. The police allowed her to do so.

In custody, Henriette was housed in a private, heated cell. She had her maid with her and was allowed special visitation privileges. She and Caillaux even dined together in the offices of the prison's director.

Her trial began three months later, on 21 July 1914, three weeks after the assassination of Archduke Franz Ferdinand that would precipitate World War One; the war itself was declared a week into the nine-day trial. But nothing as trivial as a world war would remove *L'Affaire Caillaux* from the front pages of the French newspapers. It was noted that if convicted, Henriette could face life imprisonment with hard labour or the death penalty.

The proceedings themselves jumped from scandal to scandal – Berthe Gueydan testified, revealing private details of the start of their affair, the very sort of details that Henriette had been trying to suppress. The press was captivated by Henriette's operatic fainting spells, describing with glee the way her husband "rushes, leaps and ascends the railing, to take his wife in his arms."

On 28 July, the jury retired to consider their verdict. They deliberated for less than an hour. They had been convinced by an argument made by the defence attorney, Fernand Labori.

Women, he claimed, were captive to their passions. It was literally impossible for a woman to premeditate murder; they simply did not have the capacity to do so. His client, being a female, was a person of passion, not of rationality, therefore this was a crime of passion. The jury should acquit. They did.

Henriette Caillaux walked free, and into the arms of her husband, whose honour she had somehow restored. He would continue to serve in government well into the 1920s, and in the senate until the 1940s. Henriette settled back into her life of luxury, devoting a portion of the rest of her life to the study of the sculptor Jules Dalou, writing a book about him. At the end of their lives, she and her husband were buried at the Père-Lachaise Cemetery in Paris, after a long and happy marriage.

CARIL ANN FUGATE – NATURAL BORN KILLER

"I don't know, he's kind of odd. They claim I've got him wrapped around my little finger. But I never told him to shoot anybody." – Holly Sargis in the film *Badlands*

It was a crime spree that fascinated the world – and still does. When 13-year-old Caril Ann Fugate met 18-year-old college dropout Charles Starkweather in 1956, they could not have imagined that the next two years of their lives would become the stuff of legend – turned into films, books, even a Bruce Springsteen song – and a blueprint for a certain type of American myth.

Fugate was a well-liked, intelligent student at Whittier Junior High School in Lincoln, Nebraska, when she met Starkweather. He was the friend of her sister's boyfriend, Bob Von Busch, was five years her senior and already regarded as a social misfit. He was short, bow-legged and spoke with a stammer, and his childhood had been one of bullying and violence against him. For all that, to Fugate he had a sort of animal magnetism, and the attraction was instant. They were soon inseparable.

Nobody quite knows what happened on 21 January 1958. What we do know is that Charles Starkweather went to his new girlfriend's house and shot and killed her stepfather, Marion Bartlett, and her mother, Velda. He then bludgeoned to death her two-year-old half-sister, Betty Jean.

Was Fugate there? She later claimed that she had not been, that she had come home to find Starkweather there with a gun, which he immediately pointed at her, telling her she was being held hostage and if she obeyed him, her family would be safe. Fugate also claimed that she had broken up with him shortly before, which explained his actions that day.

Whatever the truth, the pair remained in the house for six days, refusing entry to family members. Did Starkweather tell her about the murders? Did she know that he had killed once before – a gas-station attendant – on 1 December 1957? He did it, he later said, to steal $100 so they could run away together. Did she help him move the bodies to where they were later found, buried near the outbuildings of the property? According to Fugate she didn't know they were dead – is that true?

It was on the seventh day that they decided to flee, after Fugate's grandmother came by and told them if she wasn't allowed in, she would call the police. The pair fled just before the police arrived. The subsequent search of the Fugate house found no bodies – it was Starkweather's brother and Bob Von Busch who found the bodies the next day.

The pair, meanwhile, headed to Bennet, Nebraska, 2 miles away and the home of a Starkweather family friend, 70-year-old August Meyer. Starkweather broke into Meyer's gun case and stole two .22 rifles. They would be first used to shoot Meyer in the head, and secondly to shoot his dog. Fleeing the scene, Starkweather and Fugate's car became stuck in the thick January mud of Nebraska, and they decided to dump it and hitchhike. It was two local teenagers, Robert Jensen and Carol

King, who stopped to give the pair a ride. Pulling out one of the stolen rifles, Starkweather forced Jensen to drive them back to Bennet, where he led them to an abandoned storm cellar. He then shot Jensen in the head, killing him instantly.

Starkweather always admitted to killing August Meyer, the dog and Robert Jensen. But here the pair's accounts diverge. Starkweather attempted to rape King and, according to Fugate, who said she remained in Jensen's car the whole time, he became angry at failing to do it, and shot her. Starkweather said Fugate was there the whole time, and it was she who shot King.

They then drove Jensen's car to the rich part of Lincoln, breaking into the house of Chester Lauer Ward and his wife, Clara. They were out, but their maid, 51-year-old Ludmila "Lilyan" Fencl, was home. Starkweather stabbed her to death, and the pair waited for the Wards to come home. As a precaution, Starkweather broke the neck of their dog so he wouldn't alert the Wards that anything was wrong when they arrived.

Clara arrived home first. She, too, was stabbed to death – Starkweather says Fugate did it, Fugate said it was Starkweather. Soon after, Chester came home, and Starkweather shot him. Astonishingly, as they were about to leave, the Ward family's newspapers were delivered – with one front page carrying pictures of Fugate's dead family. These the pair cut out and took with them – casting suspicion on Fugate's later claim that she didn't know her family were dead. They then stole the Wards' Packard and started out for neighbouring Wyoming.

By now the police were closing in – and not just the police. The governor of Nebraska had called in the National Guard, while outraged citizens tried to take the law into their own hands, forming vigilante gangs to find and capture – or even kill – these "juvenile delinquent" killers. The pair had done little to hide their tracks – Fugate would later say Starkweather spoke to her about dying in a blaze of glory. They could hear on their own car radio that the killers – identified by name – were known to be driving a Packard with the Wards' licence plates.

The pair came across a travelling salesman, Merle Collison, who was asleep in his Buick. Again, Starkweather claims Fugate shot him, and Fugate claims it was Starkweather. A passing motorist, Joe Sprinkle, saw the commotion and stopped to see if he could help. Starkweather waved a gun at Sprinkle and then tried to drive away, but he had not used a car with a handbrake before, and the car stalled. By now another man had arrived on the scene – Natrona County sheriff's deputy, William Romer. As he did, Fugate jumped from the car and yelled to him that the driver was Charles Starkweather.

Finally releasing the handbrake, Starkweather drove away, but the car chase was short – a bullet fired into his windshield halted him. He surrendered and was arrested. Fugate was also arrested.

So, who shot who? At first both Starkweather and Fugate claimed that Starkweather was the sole killer – the most she admitted to was stealing the wallet of one of their victims. And the fact that her family were dead was news to her, she said – Starkweather had not shown her the newspaper clippings. She was simply a hostage.

The jury didn't believe her. It was noted that there were numerous opportunities for her to escape, and during the course of the trial Starkweather's testimony changed to such an extent that he was describing her as the "most trigger-happy person" he knew. If he was going to be executed, he said, then Fugate should be too.

The jury deliberated for only 22 hours before declaring Starkweather guilty, and he went to the electric chair on 25 June 1959. In a letter from prison to his parents, he wrote that he wasn't sorry for what they had done, because they had fun – Bruce Springsteen would later use this in his song about the case, "Nebraska".

Fugate was given a life sentence on 21 November 1958 and served 18 years, always protesting her innocence. A model prisoner, she was released in 1976 and set about rebuilding her life. In 2020, she was denied a pardon, which would have seen her convictions quashed.

When she was convicted, little was understood about the psychological impact of coercive control, nor of Stockholm syndrome, where a hostage comes to form an emotional bond with their captor. Did Fugate have chances to escape? Practically, the answer may be yes; emotionally and psychologically, things are less clear.

In 1973, the director Terrence Malick released *Badlands*, based on their story. It would be the first of several adaptations, from *Kalifornia* to *Natural Born Killers*, which would use the story of Fugate and Starkweather's spree as a jumping-off point. The public's fascination with the couple remains to this day.

MYRA HINDLEY – THE MOST EVIL WOMAN IN BRITAIN

Saddleworth Moor – a place of great beauty in the Peak District, in the northwest of England. Wild and desolate, it has been a huge part of the English imagination for hundreds of years as a place of strange dreams and prophecies.

But in 1965 that all changed. Any dream of Saddleworth Moor must now include the five children buried there by Myra Hindley and Ian Brady in the mid-1960s, during one of the most unusual and cruel killing sprees in history, between July 1963 and October 1965.

Hindley and Brady had met two years earlier, while both were working at a chemical distribution factory. He was 21 and she was 18. Born in 1942, Hindley had had a violent childhood, with an abusive father.

Brady already had a criminal record for theft and for threatening an ex-girlfriend with a flick knife. He was a keen reader of anything to do with the Nazis, even reading Hitler's biography *Mein Kampf*. Hindley found herself fascinated by Brady, drawn to a man who seemed so untamed – and as brutal as her father.

He took her to see porn films and they would have sex in the cinema, then go home and read to each other about Nazi atrocities – about death camps and exterminations. Hindley dyed her hair blonde and started wearing leather boots and jackets to look like Brady's Nazi ideal. Brady took pictures of Hindley in suggestive poses, dressed like a camp commandant. They began talking about carrying out the perfect murder – one that could never be solved.

On 12 July 1963, they made their first attempt at it. Fifteen-year-old Pauline Reade had been to school with Hindley's younger sister. When Brady and Hindley bumped into her on the way to a local dance, Hindley convinced her to go up to the moors with her. Hindley said she had lost a glove up there, could Reade help her find it? As she drove her up there, Brady secretly followed on his motorbike. Once there, according to Hindley, Brady led the girl away. Half an hour later, he took Hindley to where the girl's body was. She had been almost decapitated, and Brady claimed to have raped her.

In November of that same year, they snatched 12-year-old John Kilbride from a market in Ashton-under-Lyne. He too was taken up to the moors, sexually assaulted, killed and buried in a shallow grave. A huge search took place, with 2,000 volunteers scouring the local area. They didn't look on the moors, although even if they had, it seems unlikely they would have found him in that vast expanse.

In June 1964, another 12-year-old boy, Keith Bennett, went missing. He had left home to visit his grandmother. His fate was the same as John Kilbride's. Initially his stepfather was taken in for questioning, but police gradually began to link his disappearance to that of the other two children.

A fourth was to follow – ten-year-old Lesley Ann Downey. Snatched from a funfair, she was taken to Hindley's house, then stripped, raped and strangled. Brady and Hindley recorded the killing on film and tape, and when the recordings were played at the trial of the murderers, it sent the nation into shock – the fates of the children were worse than anyone had imagined. Lesley Ann Downey was also taken to the moors and buried.

The final victim was 17-year-old Edward Evans, again at Hindley's house, on 6 October 1965. Brady had been cultivating a friendship with Hindley's brother-in-law, David Smith, who was in awe of the older man. As they were killing Evans, Brady sent Hindley to go and get Smith and had them wait outside until he flashed the lights for them to come in. Entering, Smith heard a scream and found Brady hitting Evans with a hatchet, then throttling him with electrical cord. In the commotion, Brady sprained his ankle, meaning he couldn't help carry the body of the boy to the car in order to take the corpse to the moors, so he and Smith wrapped it in plastic and placed it in a spare bedroom.

If Brady thought Smith would join their "gang", he was mistaken. He arrived home, telling his wife, Hindley's sister, what he had seen. So traumatized was he that he threw up. At dawn he called the police and told them what he had witnessed. Brady was arrested for murder. At this stage, Hindley was not.

Over the next few days, more and more clues emerged linking the two to the crimes, and Hindley was arrested five days after Brady. Her mugshot would become famous – the face of "The Most Evil Woman in Britain". At the trial, both pleaded not guilty. And then the tape was played.

For 16 minutes, Lesley Ann Downey pleaded for her life with both Brady and Hindley's voices audible in the recording. The jury were also shown pornographic pictures Brady had taken of the girl, naked and tied down.

CRIMES OF PASSION

The jury only deliberated for two hours, and both Brady and Hindley ended up receiving a series of life sentences. Brady was described by the judge as "wicked beyond belief," Hindley as "a quiet, controlled, impassive witness who lied remorselessly."

Gradually, over the years, they both gave more and more details about where they had buried the bodies, with some being found and given a proper burial.

From prison, Hindley claimed that she had been an unwilling accomplice of Brady's, that he had threatened her if she didn't participate, and that she had only been playing along when he said he wanted to kill. But no one believed her, and in 1987 she offered a full confession, which put "The Most Evil Woman in Britain" back on the front pages. The mother of Lesley Ann Downey campaigned to ensure that Hindley was never released from prison, and her campaign was successful. In 2002, Hindley died of respiratory failure. Unlike her victims, it is known where she is buried. And when Ian Brady died in 2017, the last chance of finding all of them died too.

CAROLYN WARMUS – A FATAL ATTRACTION

She was not the normal profile for a killer – her childhood had known no deprivation, there was nothing obvious that she had to be angry about. Her father, Thomas A. Warmus, was a self-made multimillionaire, his insurance business allowing him to own eight jets, two yachts and 15 cars, plus property dotted around the US. When he and his wife divorced in 1970, their daughter was six, and while the custody battle had been bitter, she still enjoyed a cosseted life.

After she graduated from school, she went to the University of Michigan, studying psychology and then education. In 1987, at the age of 23, she took a job at Greenville Elementary School in Scarsdale, New York, and met Paul Solomon.

He was a fifth-grade teacher, 17 years older than Warmus and married to Betty Jeanne. They had a teenage daughter, Kristan. Warmus and Solomon were attracted to each other and soon began an affair, with Solomon assuring Warmus that he would leave his wife as soon as Kristan was old enough to move out.

What Solomon didn't know was that his heiress lover had some past experience with older – and as her friends later told police – unattainable men. While at university, she had fallen for teaching assistant Paul Laven, who broke things off with her to become engaged. Soon after, it is alleged that Warmus regularly broke into their apartment, leaving notes for them and breaking things. The couple were granted a restraining order against Warmus, made permanent after their wedding. They were relieved when she moved to New York.

On 15 January 1989, Warmus and Solomon had drinks together, and then moved to his car for sex – one of the few places where they could do so. Then they parted company, and Solomon returned home. What he found horrified him. His wife lay dead on the floor in a pool of blood. She had been pistol-whipped and shot nine times.

Police immediately linked the murder to a phone call they had received from a woman in distress earlier that night – the call had broken off before they were able to establish an address. Solomon was immediately the main suspect, but he was able to supply an alibi for the time of that call – he had gone bowling with friends, before meeting up with Warmus. His friends were able to confirm his presence with them.

Solomon's lawyer recommended that he break all ties with Warmus, which he did, and shortly after, he found a new girlfriend. Warmus disappeared from his life, and the trail of the killer had gone cold. No link could be found to his ex-lover – the police wrote the death of his wife off as a random attack.

Five months later, Solomon and his new girlfriend went on holiday to Puerto Rico. Unbeknown to them, so did Carolyn Warmus.

Warmus had, it would turn out, already contacted the family of Solomon's new girlfriend, pretending to be a police officer, and urged them to stop the relationship. When she turned up in Puerto Rico, Solomon contacted the police. Suddenly the case they thought had gone cold had heated up again – could it be that Solomon's former lover had killed Betty Jeanne? Where was Warmus before she met up with Solomon, at the time when they received the distress call?

It was soon established that Warmus had obtained a .25 Beretta pistol with a silencer shortly before the murder, using a stolen driver's licence. It was the same gun used to kill Betty Jeanne. In addition, on top of the restraining order against her at university, it turned out that she had previously hired a private detective to find incriminating material on a married bartender whose relationship she hoped to break up. She was arrested in February 1990, and her trial – which became known as the "Fatal Attraction trial", after the 1987 film – began in January 1991.

The defence argued that there was only circumstantial evidence linking her to the killing – the gun purchase, the affair, her past actions – and none put her definitively at the scene of the crime. The jury could not reach a unanimous verdict, and the judge called a mistrial.

A year later, new evidence emerged. Solomon submitted a bloody cashmere glove belonging to Warmus, which he had found at the house three years after his wife's death and failed to submit previously. Warmus had never been there with him – the only time she could have been there was the night of the killing.

This time the jury was able to hand down a unanimous verdict, and the judge imposed a maximum life sentence on her. She continued to plead her innocence, saying that if she was guilty of anything, it was being foolish enough to believe the lies and promises that Paul Solomon made to her.

CRIMES OF PASSION

Her attorney offered a reward of $250,000 for any information that would lead to the arrest of the "true killer" of Betty Jeanne. It was never claimed.

Carolyn Warmus served 25 years, and was released in July 2019. She has continued to maintain her innocence and her stated position that she was framed by Solomon to cover for his infidelity. The glove has never been DNA tested, for reasons that remain a mystery.

KELLY COCHRAN – THE PACT

Their pact was simple. Kelly Gaboyan and Jason Cochran met at high school in Merrillville, Indiana and fell in love, and when they married each other in 2002, they made a deal that would have horrific consequences. They promised each other that they would kill anyone that they cheated with.

For the next ten years, Jason Cochran worked installing swimming pools, and the pair seemed to have a happy marriage. But then Jason's back gave out, the work dried up, and the pair lost their house and were forced to move. They headed to Michigan, where they could live more cheaply, and in the hope of finding a source of legal marijuana for Jason's back pain.

Kelly took on full-time factory work, and it was there that she met Christopher Regan. At 53, he was some twenty years her senior. Tired of dealing with her incapacitated husband, Kelly started an affair with Regan.

No one knows how Jason found out about it – but he did. Nor do we know if he reminded Kelly of the pact, or how she reacted. But on 14 October 2014, Kelly invited Regan to her home for sex. It was the first time he had gone to the Cochran house. He would never leave.

It was Regan's own girlfriend, Terri O'Donnell, who reported him missing ten days later. Suspicions had already been raised about his absence from work – he was known to be a diligent employee who rarely, if ever, missed a shift. Police investigations failed to find the missing man – they did question Kelly, who admitted to the affair, but there was no evidence. Jason, in the role of jealous husband, was the chief suspect, but nothing could be found to pin on him. The case was declared cold.

That was, until 20 February 2016, when medics were called to a house in Hobart, Indiana, where the Cochrans had moved after the disappearance of Christopher Regan. A man – Jason Cochran – was found unresponsive, having taken a suspected overdose of heroin. Attempts to revive him were unsuccessful, and, as the emergency service team said afterwards, were hampered by his wife, who proved to be extremely agitated and disruptive.

Two days later, Kelly held a memorial service for her dead husband, which she described as the hardest thing she had done in her life, and then she fled. The next day, the autopsy results came in. Jason had not died of a heroin overdose – he had been asphyxiated, and only Kelly could have done it.

She was now on the run. Astonishingly, she stayed in touch with the police investigating her husband's death – she thought texting them false addresses would fool them, but they simply traced the phone. On 29 April 2016, she was arrested and charged with murder.

It was then that the police found out about the horrific death of Christopher Regan. The couple's pact had stayed strong – when Jason found out about Kelly's affair, he made her invite Regan over to the house. As she had promised, Kelly took him to bed. And while they were having sex, Jason Cochran shot Regan in the head.

The couple then dismembered the body. Neighbours confirmed that on the night of the disappearance they had heard a gunshot, and then the sound of power tools. If that wasn't traumatic enough, some neighbours also reported having attended a barbecue at the couple's house soon after, at which they were served copious amounts of meat...

Why did Kelly kill Jason? In her telling, she did it out of revenge. In fact, on the night they killed Regan, she had contemplated killing her invalid husband instead. But just before that, Regan had told her he didn't want a serious relationship with her. So she had decided to invoke the pact.

Since that night, she had grown to hate her husband more and more. Eventually she could stand it no longer, and after making him comatose with heroin, she had smothered him. She told investigators that she had evened the score.

During questioning, Kelly's story changed several times. Sometimes she claimed she had no part in Regan's killing, saying she was tied up when Jason killed and dismembered her lover; sometimes she insisted that she had killed even more men – another nine by her telling. No evidence of this has ever been found but it didn't need to be to put her away. Kelly Cochran was given a 65-year sentence for the killing of her husband, and will never be released.

MARY PEARCEY – JACK THE RIPPER?

Who was Jack the Ripper? The list of suspects remains vast, running to well over 100 names. From the son of King Edward VII, Prince Albert; to the painter Walter Sickert; to the cigar manufacturer Hyam Hyams; to the Russian conman Michael Ostrog – there remains a rogue's gallery of potential Jacks. Even Lewis Carroll, the author of *Alice's Adventures in Wonderland*, has been suggested by amateur sleuths.

But only one woman has ever seriously been considered as a female candidate for Jack the Ripper. Her name was Mary Pearcey, and she went to the gallows in 1890, two days before Christmas, for the murder of her lover's wife and daughter.

She had been born Mary Eleanor Wheeler in 1866, taking the name Pearcey from a carpenter she lived with, who left her because of her infidelities. Soon after, she moved in with a furniture maker, Frank Hogg. Hogg was also involved with another woman, Phoebe Styles, which was no secret from Pearcey. In fact, when Styles fell pregnant, Pearcey selflessly urged Hogg to make an honest woman of her by marrying her. This he did, and soon after their daughter was born, whom they also named Phoebe, although she was known as Tiggy.

Pearcey's selflessness didn't last long. On 24 October 1890, she summoned Phoebe Styles and her 18-month-old daughter to her home in London's Hampstead. Neighbours would later report hearing screaming. That evening, a corpse was found in a nearby rubbish heap. It had a crushed skull, which had nearly been severed from the neck.

A mile away was an empty pram, with bloodstained cushions inside it. A huge hunt ensued, and the next morning, the body of a toddler was found in nearby Finchley. It had been smothered and thrown into a waste ground.

It was soon evident to police that Phoebe's husband had not been a faithful one, and suspicion immediately grew around his lover, Mary Pearcey. Her home was immediately searched. If Pearcey had been indiscreet about her relationship with Hogg, she was even less so regarding the murders she committed. Her kitchen showed signs of a struggle and was covered in bloodstains. The police also found an axe, two knives and a poker covered in blood, a clump of bloodied hair, and love letters between Pearcey and Hogg. The whole time they were searching her house, Pearcey sat at a piano, playing and singing loudly.

On questioning, Pearcey claimed that the blood came from her trying to kill mice – "Killing mice, killing mice, killing mice!" was what she screamed at the police. Unsurprisingly, the story was not believed, and she was charged with murder. During the subsequent trial, it became evident that the mother had been killed first, and then her body thrown on top of the pram, suffocating the child.

The trial was brief – the jury found her guilty and she was sentenced to be hanged.

CRIMES OF PASSION

The bloodiness of the case caused a sensation. Madame Tussauds waxworks immediately made a model of Pearcey, and its first day of being on display drew 30,000 people.

Pearcey was stoical as she waited to be hanged. The police had, she said, come to the right conclusions, but a good deal of evidence they'd used was false. Her hanging was, by the account of the hangman, "quiet and painless." The noose was preserved and is still displayed in New Scotland Yard.

It was Arthur Conan Doyle, the author of the Sherlock Holmes books, who first put forward the theory that Jack the Ripper may have been a woman. He noted that the only people seen on the London streets with blood on their clothes were midwives – might this not be the perfect alibi for a murderer? He didn't name Pearcey, but her fame, and the horror of her deeds, meant that in the popular imagination she became an obvious candidate.

As with so many Jack the Ripper suspects, the evidence was only ever circumstantial, and it seems clear that the murders Pearcey actually carried out had a motive – she was no random killer. And it is now generally held that the sheer amount of physical violence associated with the Ripper's killings make it much more likely that the killer was a man – a woman of that sort of strength was rare in Victorian London.

And yet – in 2006, the letters the Ripper purportedly sent to newspapers with details of the bloody crimes were DNA tested. The saliva on them, used to lick the stamps, contained a surprise. It was that of a woman…

YOLANDA SALDÍVAR – KILLER FAN

Love comes in many colours. When does affection turn into obsession, and when does obsession turn into murder?

Selena Quintanilla-Pérez, known simply as Selena, was famous for being the Queen of Tejano Music, with *Billboard* listing her third in their Greatest of All Time: Latin Artists list, behind only Enrique Iglesias and Luis Miguel.

Born in Texas in 1971 to a Mexican family, her first band was made up of her and her older siblings. Soon after, she went solo, courting controversy by performing Tejano music, usually the domain of men. But by the age of 17, she was topping the charts and winning awards, including at the Grammys. Her fan base grew and grew, her albums became bestsellers and her future seemed bright.

Yolanda Saldívar was a big fan. One of seven children, she was 11 years older than Selena and had worked as a nurse. She loved Selena's music, and after seeing one of her concerts, she called the singer's father and proposed setting up a fan club. He wasn't sure – who was this woman? – but the calls were persistent, and he eventually gave in. Saldívar became the president of the club.

CRIMES OF PASSION

Soon after, Selena asked Saldívar to run the luxury boutiques and beauty salons she had set up in her name, "Selena Etc.". The fan club continued to grow in size, and the boutiques made a healthy profit. And yet…

Fans started contacting Selena's father, telling him they had paid for subscriptions and received nothing. At the boutiques, staff kept being sacked for no apparent reason, except that Saldívar didn't like them – they were not replaced, but the wage bills remained the same.

Close investigation of the finances of both the club and the boutiques in 1995 revealed holes in the profits. Suspicion immediately fell on Saldívar, and in the first week of March of that year she was sacked for embezzlement. Selena's parents threatened to involve the police if Saldívar failed to hand over outstanding cash and the financial records. Saldívar said she would only do so personally to Selena. A meeting was arranged on 31 March at a hotel in South Texas.

What happened next seems like a farce. When Selena arrived, Saldívar was in tears and claimed she had been raped in Mexico on the way to the hotel. Selena took her to a local hospital, but she was refused an examination as the alleged assault had occurred over the border. The pair then returned to the hotel.

Had Saldívar already decided to kill Selena? Was the rape story a delaying tactic? Did she think she could not go through with it? Whatever she was thinking, when they got back to the hotel, she drew a .38 Taurus Model 85 revolver out of her handbag and aimed it at Selena. The singer tried to flee, but Saldívar shot her in the right lower shoulder, severing an artery and causing a severe loss of blood. Selena kept running, making it as far as the hotel lobby, leaving a trail of blood. She was seen clutching her chest screaming, "Help me! Help me!

I've been shot!" Saldívar chased after her, raising the gun and calling her a "bitch".

She collapsed at reception. The clerk called emergency services and she was rushed back to the same hospital she had been to earlier. Although she still had a weak heartbeat, surgeons were unable to resuscitate her, and she was declared dead at 1.05 p.m., an hour and a half after she had been shot. At her funeral some 40,000 people passed her casket, and 78,000 signed the condolence book.

Saldívar had attempted to escape in a pickup truck, but she was soon surrounded. A 10-hour stand-off ensued, during which she repeatedly aimed the gun at her own head, threatening to shoot herself. She finally surrendered and was charged with first-degree murder.

The trial was a huge media event. Saldívar argued that she had not meant to kill Selena – she had actually planned to kill herself in front of her hero, but the gun went off accidentally. Other witnesses testified that there had been four previous occasions where Saldívar had planned to kill the singer, only being stopped by circumstances. In the end she was sentenced to the maximum sentence of life imprisonment, with no eligibility for parole for 30 years. She was also placed on suicide watch and kept far from other prisoners, who made death threats – there was even a reward offered among fellow inmates for her murder.

Was her killing of Selena simply an attempt to escape from the embezzlement charges she might face? As the trial progressed, more and more details of her obsession with the singer came out. Saldívar's house was covered in pictures of Selena, and she had a whole video library of the singer she would play to visitors. She even had a shrine set up, where she would burn votive candles. She told people she wanted to be just like her idol, even dressing like her. As their business relationship failed, and other people began to take over the books, Saldívar became more and more angry at her hero, and jealous of her new managers. She felt betrayed. If she could not have Selena, no one else could.

Many fans loved Selena – but only one fan took her obsession to the point where love became hate, with deadly consequences. Selena's birthday, two weeks after her death, was declared "Selena Day" by then governor of Texas, George W. Bush.

EVELYN DICK – THE SOCIALITE – AND SOCIOPATH?

It was a trial that captivated Canada. Known for her beauty and her socializing, Evelyn Dick was born in Ontario in 1920 to Scottish immigrants Donald and Alexandra MacLean. Her father was an alcoholic who collected firearms. He also committed fraud, embezzling nearly $200,000 from his employer, the Hamilton Street Railway (HSR).

She moved in upper-class circles and was known to have many lovers, so it was a surprise when, in 1945, aged 24, she married John Dick, another HSR employee – a lowly conductor. At some point, Dick presented his wife with evidence of her father's theft – some think he had done this earlier to blackmail her into marrying him. He had little money – it was Evelyn who bought their house.

It certainly didn't seem a close marriage – within days of tying the knot, Evelyn started seeing another man, Bill Bohozuk. No one was surprised when, three months later, John and Evelyn Dick separated. Nothing more was heard of John.

CRIMES OF PASSION

On 16 March 1946, a group of five children were playing in the woods near where the couple had lived and made a horrific discovery. What they initially thought was the body of a pig, hidden among the trees, turned out to be the naked body of a man. All the limbs were missing, sawn off, as had been the head. The corpse was soon identified as John Dick – Alexander Kammerer, Dick's cousin, had reported him missing on 6 March.

Evelyn, her father, who the police also suspected was involved, and Bill Bohozuk were all arrested and charged with murder. Bohozuk was acquitted, despite his lover's attempts to frame him for the murder. Donald MacLean was found to be an accessory to the murder and given four years. But it was the details about Evelyn Dick that turned the trial into a sensation.

Evelyn had kept a little black book of her sexual encounters, and some 150 men were listed as having had sex with her. Most were wealthy socialites, many of them married, and she boasted that they included the son of the judge in the trial.

When questioned about the murder of her husband, she said not to look at her, she didn't know anything about it. And yet at the time of the killing she had borrowed a car from a friend and returned it with bloodstains on the seats. The blood matched John's. She then told a story about a Mafia hitman who had found out John was sleeping with his wife and killed him. She was unable to present any evidence pointing to this.

By then, police had searched her house and yard and had found, in an outside furnace, the missing body parts of her husband, burned down to their bones. The trial lasted only nine days, and the jury took less than two hours to reach a guilty verdict. Evelyn Dick was sentenced to hang.

However, soon after, she was acquitted on appeal – the grounds were misdirection by the trial judge, and statements by the respondent, while in custody, wrongly admitted in evidence. She was released from prison, and the murder verdict was quashed. It was then that things took an even more horrific turn.

Another search of her house had found something no one had been looking for – the body of an infant encased in cement and placed in a suitcase under the floorboards. She was arrested and put on trial again. During the court case, it became known that she had given birth to three children, giving the father's name each time as the fictitious "Norman White". The children were Peter, Heather and another girl who died in childbirth. The body beneath the floorboards was identified as Peter; he had died at 18 months of age.

Evelyn was again arrested, and again pleaded innocent. Again, the jury didn't believe her. She was sentenced to life in prison. She served only 11 years – it is said that certain of those well-connected men from her black book may have helped engineer her release. Freed in 1958, she disappeared – never to be heard of again.

Did Evelyn kill her husband and child, Peter? Doubts have emerged since. Psychological examination at the time seemed to suggest she had the mental capacity of a 13-year-old girl, which was perhaps brought about by the abuse by her alcoholic father. On top of that, Evelyn's mother claimed she had seen her husband with the suitcase they found Peter in soon before the boy went missing, and he had told her to "get the hell out" of the room. Could it be that Evelyn's father was the true killer of both John and Peter? Is that why Evelyn tried to frame Bill Bohozuk, to protect her father, as she had protected him by marrying John Dick in the first place? Was this an act of love?

CRIMES OF PASSION

Whatever the truth, Evelyn Dick – the murderer – has been immortalized in a Canadian schoolyard chant, and the missing word is not hard to guess...
You cut off his legs...
You cut off his arms...
You cut off his head...
You cut off his...
How could you, Mrs Dick?
How could you, Mrs Dick?

ROSEMARY WEST – HORROR IN SUBURBIA

It was the case that shocked Britain. It began in 1992. A concerned mother called the police and informed them that her daughter's schoolfriend had told her daughter that she had been raped. That schoolfriend was Louise West, daughter of Rosemary and Fred West, and the person who had raped her, Louise told her friend, was her father. Police swept into the Wests' house in Gloucestershire and arrested Fred. What they did not know was that the house had been used for a lot more than the sexual assault of Louise. It would soon become known as the "House of Horrors".

Rosemary West was born in Devon, UK, in 1953, the fifth of seven children in a poor family. Her mother suffered from depression and had undergone electroconvulsive therapy while pregnant with Rose. Some believe this may have affected the mental development of her child. Her father suffered from paranoid schizophrenia and regularly sexually assaulted Rose and her older sister Patricia, also carrying out acts of extreme violence against them. From the age of 13, Rose, in turn, was known to sexually molest her nine-year-old brother, Graham, climbing into his bed naked and assaulting him.

She was sitting at a bus stop aged 15 when she met Fred West, then 27. Initially repulsed by him, she soon found herself enjoying the attention he lavished on her. At the time she worked in a bread shop, and Fred was soon picking her up and taking her to the caravan park where he lived with his two children from his first marriage. They decided that Rose would become the full-time nanny of eight-year-old Anne Marie and five-year-old Charmaine, and in return Fred would give her the same money as the bread shop had, so she could pretend to her parents she still worked there.

When her parents found out, they contacted social services about West, and in 1969, 15-year-old Rose was placed in a home for troubled teenagers. On her release at the age of 16, she immediately returned to Fred.

Within weeks she was pregnant and later gave birth to a daughter, Heather. While Fred served time for theft, she looked after the three girls. Anne Marie and Charmaine would later tell of the physical and emotional abuse they suffered at the hands of the woman they were forced to call "Mummy". They would be tied naked and beaten with a wooden spoon for the smallest infraction.

It was shortly before Fred's release that Rose killed Charmaine, storing her body in a coal cellar. On his release, Fred buried her in the garden, the first of many corpses that would fill the suburban back yard. The couple told everyone that Charmaine's mother had come and picked her up.

Her mother had in fact come to their house in Much Marcle, Gloucestershire, but she had never returned to her own home. Her body was found later, dismembered and placed in plastic bags. There was evidence that she had been sexually assaulted with a steel pole before being killed.

By now, Rose and Fred were married. Eight-year-old Anne Marie was regularly being raped and beaten by the couple. By 13, she had been forced into prostitution. But when her sister Louise told her schoolfriend about the situation and the police approached the Wests, the case fell apart, as they were too scared to testify.

Rose's daughter, Heather, born in 1970, was missing, as was another woman Fred had made pregnant in 1967, Anne McFall. The Wests had also been charged, in 1973, with the sexual assault of their children's nanny, Caroline Owens. Again, they had walked free, with Owens attempting suicide shortly after.

But the 1992 rape case, although dropped, revealed that Heather, the Wests' first of five children together – Rose had three others with clients as a prostitute – had been missing since 1987. During pre-trial questioning, Anne Marie had told the police that it was a "family joke" that her half-sister Heather was buried beneath the patio of the house.

On 23 February 1994, the police obtained a search warrant and permission to excavate the patio area. As they began digging, Fred West changed his story. Having claimed Heather had simply left home, he admitted he had killed her "in a fit of rage", then dismembered her and stored her in a dustbin, before burying her in the garden. Rose had no knowledge of this, he said.

Three days later the police found a thigh bone and a pile of fingernails, which could only have been removed as a form of torture. Fred West was arrested for the murder of his daughter. But the case was not closed – a third thigh bone was soon discovered, pointing to more than one victim. And then more. The police obtained permission to dig up the entire yard. And the bodies kept coming.

CRIMES OF PASSION

West confessed to what he said were "approximately nine murders". The figure was definitely approximate – in all, 12 bodies were found. Each one had been mutilated, and all 12 showed signs of extreme sexual abuse prior to the murder. Many had adhesive tape wrapped around the head with straws pushed into the nostrils to allow the victim to breathe during the abuse, and most were missing fingers and toes. The cellar at the West house had been a torture chamber.

Despite pleas of innocence, Rose was also charged with nine murder counts. Evidence from their children made it clear that she had participated fully in Fred's sexual abuse of them, often tying them down for her husband, and delivering beatings and torture. At her trial, Rose West claimed that she was simply a grieving mother who had been married to a monster. She also pointed to the fact that Fred had killed women before they met, using the same methods.

She went to trial on 3 October 1995. On New Year's Day that same year, Fred had managed to hang himself in his cell. Only Rose would face justice.

The evidence of Rose's sexual sadism and her involvement in the murders was overwhelming. The judge informed the jury that even if Fred West had done the actual killing, under the law, if two people participate in a murder, they are equally guilty. Accordingly, on 22 November 1995, Rose West was found guilty of ten of the murders and sentenced to life imprisonment without the possibility of parole – the first woman to receive that sentence in the UK.

The house at 25 Cromwell Street was demolished and is now a public pathway. The "House of Horrors" has been replaced by a peaceful green track leading into the centre of town and away from the crimes that made it famous.

53

CHARLENE GALLEGO – SEX-SLAVE KILLER

They met in a poker club in Sacramento. It was 1977, Gerald Gallego was 31 and she was ten years younger. Charlene had a reputation that preceded her – according to locals she was a nymphomaniac who loved heroin.

Born in 1956, she had been married and divorced twice. Gerald had also been married; in fact, he was married when he met Charlene. Within a week they were living together, and enjoying BDSM (bondage, discipline, sadism, masochism), with Charlene as the subservient partner. They married soon after – not for the first or last time, Gerald married a woman without divorcing the last one.

It was a few months later that Gerald brought home another woman, a 16-year-old exotic dancer. They had a threesome, and Gerald left for work the next morning. When he returned, he found the two women still in bed together, having sex. In a fury, he beat Charlene and threw the other girl out of the window, so she made her escape. Later, however, they reconciled, and it was decided that they would work together to satisfy Gerald's lusts. He needed slaves, and Charlene would help him get them.

CRIMES OF PASSION

On 10 September 1978, 16-year-old Kippi Vaught and 17-year-old Rhonda Scheffler were shopping in Sacramento's Country Club Plaza, when Gerald approached them with a gun. Bundled into a van driven by Charlene, the two victims were taken to the home of the Gallegos in Baxter, California, then repeatedly assaulted by Gerald all through the night.

The next day, Gerald and Charlene marched the girls to a field and beat them with a tyre iron. Then, he pulled out a .25 pistol and shot each girl once in the head. Vaught didn't die from the initial gunshot and started to try and crawl away. Gerald shot her in the head three more times. Charlene would later admit she felt overwhelming sexual pleasure as the girls died.

Six months later, 14-year-old Brenda Judd and 13-year-old Sandra Colley were abducted from a local fair in Nevada and thrown into the back of the van. Charlene drove the Interstate 80, watching in the rear-view mirror and masturbating as Gerald repeatedly assaulted the girls. They parked at a desolate area known as Humboldt Sink, and Charlene made the girls perform sex acts on each other as Gerald watched. He then took Colley away to a dry creek bed, carrying a shovel. Charlene heard what she later described as a loud splat, the girl sank to her knees and slowly toppled onto her face. He then beat Judd to death. The pair buried the girls naked in the same grave.

On 24 April 1980, they decided they needed another slave. Driving around Nevada, they saw Stacy Redican and Karen Chipman-Twiggs, both 17, leaving a bookstore. They picked them up with the promise of marijuana. In the van, as Charlene drove, Gerald made them undress, then sexually assaulted both of them as Charlene drove. They took them to a remote area, and Gerald killed each of them with a hammer.

Worse was to follow, as their crimes grew more brutal. On 6 June 1980, they abducted 21-year-old Linda Teresa Aguilar, who was four months pregnant. When her body was discovered on 22 June, her wrists and ankles were bound with nylon cord and her skull was broken. Investigators discovered that her mouth was full of sand, meaning she had been buried alive, either by accident or on purpose – either way, it was a horrifying death.

Their next victim was known to them – 31-year-old Virginia Mochel, a bartender in a place where they often drank. Virginia was sexually assaulted by Gerald, who then forced her to beg for her life. She was found three months later, with strangulation marks around her neck.

It was the next killing that would see them apprehended. On 1 November, 22-year-old Craig Miller and his fiancée, 21-year-old Mary Elizabeth Sowers, were kidnapped, with Gerald pointing a gun at them. They took them to a remote location and Gerald shot Miller three times by the side of the road, forcing Sowers to watch. Then they took her home and sexually assaulted her, before shooting her three times in the head.

But their van had been identified. Gerald was at a Western Union office, collecting money Charlene's parents had sent her, when the police burst in. He was charged with the last two murders, as was Charlene. Charlene turned state witness, testifying against her husband in order to receive a reduced sentence. She got 16 years. Gerald Gallego got death, but died before he could be executed, of rectal cancer, in 2002.

Charlene Gallego served her sentence and was released in 1997. She claimed that she was also a victim. She also claimed that she had tried to save some of their lives. She never produced any evidence that she did.

GAIL COLLINS PAPPALARDI – STRANGE BREW

The song was good, Eric Clapton knew that, but something was missing. It was called "Lawdy Mama", and the plan was to include it on the Cream album *Disraeli Gears*, but Clapton could not make it work. He handed it over to the album's producer, Felix Pappalardi, to see what he could do with it. Felix set about transforming the sound of it and passed the lyrics on to his then girlfriend, Gail Collins, to rewrite. She did, and the 1967 hit song "Strange Brew" was born.

Felix Pappalardi and Gail Collins were legends in the rock scene at the time. Pappalardi's own band, Mountain, hit the charts with its song "Mississippi Queen", but he was most closely associated with Cream, as well as producing folk singers such as Joan Baez and Buffy Sainte-Marie.

He and Collins married in June 1969, and theirs was a life of excess. She was a poet and artist and would write most of Mountain's lyrics and create the artwork for their album covers, while Felix wrote the music and played bass. She was from Maryland, and by her own account had married young and had two sons, whereabouts unknown. She met Felix in 1964, soon after he had left music school and fallen in love with the Greenwich Village folk scene. The pair became inseparable.

As Mountain – regarded as a precursor to heavy metal music with their incredibly loud songs – became increasingly successful, she exerted more and more control over the group. Fellow member Leslie West blamed her for the band's demise. "Felix's wife got in the way of everything," West complained. "She just wanted too much control of the group." Felix never denied their relationship was tempestuous, telling a reporter that they would argue about everything – except music. "Me and my old lady fight, but never about that," he said. "That's always straight ahead."

Mountain's success left them both very wealthy – and Felix almost deaf. With no need to work any more, the pair gave themselves over to a life of sex and drugs – and guns. Felix was known to drive the streets in a Rolls-Royce, firing at glass windows, street signs and telephone booths. The former drummer in Mountain, Corky Laing, said he always knew it would end in tragedy of one sort or another. "Felix's death was inevitable," he told crime writer David J. Krajicek. He pointed out that Felix had guns and substance-abuse problems, as well as emotional ones. "When you've got that combination, something is going to happen."

As with so many on the scene, the pair had an open relationship, and things didn't always go smoothly. Collins said he sometimes minded her seeing other people, and she sometimes minded him doing the same – proof, she said, that life is not always perfect.

On 17 April 1983, life became very imperfect indeed. The police were called to an apartment in Manhattan. There, they found Felix Pappalardi dead in bed, wearing only his underwear. He had been shot once in the neck. Collins, who had called them, was also there, still cradling the Deringer gun her husband had bought her only a few weeks before. And on a table in the apartment was their marriage certificate – shredded.

Felix had been seeing a young singer and had returned in the early hours of the morning. According to Collins this was nothing unusual, and she said that the gun had gone off when he was showing her how to use it. She admitted that she had recently told her friends the marriage was in trouble. She was also forced to admit that it did seem odd that she had phoned her attorney before she called the police.

Collins was tried for second-degree murder. The prosecutors pointed out that she had carried a gun for years, so her story that her husband was showing her how to use it stretched credibility.

She was, though, acquitted of second-degree murder and manslaughter. But they found her guilty of criminally negligent homicide and sentenced her to four years in prison. Released on parole in 1985, she spent the rest of her life in Mexico, living with her cats. On her death, she and the cats were cremated, and their ashes mixed together – a strange end to a strange life.

SUSAN ATKINS, PATRICIA KRENWINKEL AND LESLIE VAN HOUTEN – THE MANSON FAMILY

When did the Summer of Love end? For some it was the Altamont Free Concert on 6 December, where Hells Angels were deployed as security guards and killed a man during the Rolling Stones set. But for many others, the hippie era was officially over in early August of that year, after two horrific nights of murders carried out by the followers of Charles Manson – the Manson Family.

At its peak, the Family had nearly 100 members, devoted to their leader, Charles Manson, whom they believed to be a manifestation of Jesus, preparing his followers for a race war to come. They lived a life of hippie excess, with lots of drugs and sex. But if these things had meant peace and love in 1967, they were about to mean war and hate in 1969.

On 8 August, Manson gathered three of his female followers together – Susan Atkins, Patricia Krenwinkel and Linda Kasabian. With fellow cult leader Tex Watson, they were to go to the house of the film director Roman Polanski on Cielo Drive, and do whatever Tex told them to. Watson had been told by Manson to destroy everyone they found there and to be as gruesome as he could.

The four drove to the house, arriving just after midnight and encountering in the driveway Steven Parent, driving home from visiting the caretaker William Garretson. Watson stabbed him in the face and shot him four times in the chest. Watson, Atkins and Krenwinkel then left Kasabian to guard the entrance as they broke into the house.

Inside the house was Polanski's wife, the actress Sharon Tate, who was eight months pregnant. Also there were her friend and former lover Jay Sebring, Polanski's friend Wojciech Frykowski and his girlfriend, Abigail Folger, heiress to the Folgers coffee fortune. Absent were Polanski, who was away working, and the music producer Quincy Jones, who had planned to be there but cancelled at the last moment.

Frykowski was asleep on the couch. Watson woke him with a kick in the head. Then Tate, Sebring and Folger were dragged to the living room. Watson tied Tate and Sebring together around their necks, and when Sebring protested Watson shot him seven times. Atkins stabbed Frykowski in the leg several times, and then Watson shot him twice.

Folger attempted to escape, running from the house, but was chased down by Krenwinkel, who restrained her as she and Watson stabbed her 28 times, and Frykowski, who had survived the gunshots, 51 times. They then went back inside, where Tate was still alive.

She begged them not to kill her until the baby was born, offering to be their hostage until then. But she too was stabbed, 16 times. Still alive, she was hanged next to Sebring, who had died before they strung him up. As they left, Atkins wrote "PIG" on the outside wall in Tate's blood.

The next night, with their first victims still undiscovered, the same foursome, plus Manson himself, Clem Grogan and Leslie Van Houten, drove to 3301 Waverly Drive in the Los Feliz section of Los Angeles – the home of Leno and Rosemary LaBianca. Manson went ahead and found Leno on the couch, and tied his hands. Rosemary was in a bedroom and she was also secured. Pillowcases were placed over their heads and secured with cords. Watson, Krenwinkel and Van Houten then went into the house, as the others, including Manson, headed off to Venice Beach.

In the living room, Watson used a bayonet to stab Leno 12 times. In the bedroom, Krenwinkel stabbed Rosemary again and again with a kitchen knife, which she then handed to Van Houten. Van Houten had not been at the previous night's spree. Now she stabbed Rosemary 16 times in the back and buttocks. Krenwinkel then used the LaBiancas' blood to write "Rise" and "Death to pigs" on the walls and "Healter [sic] Skelter" on the refrigerator door.

It was not until 19 hours later that the bodies were discovered, when Rosemary's 15-year-old son from a previous marriage returned home. Initially, the LAPD dismissed any connection between the two murder scenes.

It was only sheer chance that saw the Manson Family caught. The police had been investigating stolen cars, which Manson and his followers had been converting into dune buggies. Twenty family members were arrested, and Atkins' housemate told them about their involvement in the killings. Atkins soon confessed, and the grisly details became public.

At the trial, Linda Kasabian was granted immunity, as she had not carried out any of the killings. She turned state witness and her evidence was damning. Manson, Atkins and Krenwinkel were charged with seven counts of murder, Van Houten with two. Watson had initially escaped; when he was later arrested, he too was charged with seven murders. All five Family members were sentenced to death. But before the death sentence could be carried out, the Supreme Court of California ruled that the state's death-penalty laws were unconstitutional. Some 107 inmates were spared, including Manson and his followers.

The three women – Susan Atkins, Patricia Krenwinkel and Leslie Van Houten, had their death sentences commuted to life behind bars. Atkins, the daughter of two alcoholic parents, was known as quiet and self-conscious until she met Manson. She helped him with an earlier killing, that of Gary Hinman, whose large inheritance Manson hoped to steal. Her evidence in the court case for the later sprees was detailed – when Sharon Tate begged for the life of her baby, Atkins had said that she had no mercy for her and that she had stabbed her because she was sick of listening to her, pleading and begging, begging and pleading. She died in prison in 2009, having become a born-again Christian and been married twice while incarcerated.

Patricia Krenwinkel had considered becoming a nun when she was 17. At 20 she met Manson, and they had sex that night – he was, she said, the first man to tell her she was beautiful. After helping to kill the LaBiancas, she spent time playing with their dogs. In prison she received a bachelor's degree in human services from the University of La Verne, and set up Alcoholics Anonymous and Narcotics Anonymous groups. She was granted parole in 2022, but the state governor overturned the decision, and she remained in jail.

More fortunate was Leslie Van Houten – after 25 parole hearings, five of which found in her favour, and four of which were reversed, she was released on 11 July 2023. Having started experimenting with drugs at the age of 14, she took LSD for the first time a year later. She dropped out and at the age of 19 joined Manson's commune. Manson kept her and many of his followers dosed up on hallucinogens, leading to psychotic episodes, and Van Houten claims she was "saturated in acid" when she did the killings.

At the time of writing, she is the only member of the Manson Family to be paroled – Tex Watson had been denied parole 17 times up to 2021, and Manson himself died in prison in 2017. At the parole hearing, Van Houten told the board that she had spent all those years returning to being a decent human being – like she was before meeting the depraved Charles Manson.

MARIETTE BOSCH – DEATH IN BOTSWANA

It was a strange and unreal world they moved in, and it was about to get stranger. When Mariette and Justin Bosch moved to Botswana in 1992, they were attracted by the white enclave that fellow expatriates had set up around the capital Gaborone. Here the Boschs, who had emigrated from South Africa, were able to afford a lifestyle far beyond what they could have in their home country. A maid, a servant, a gardener – these things were out of reach in South Africa, but de rigueur for the white population they moved among in their new home country.

Fifty-year-old Mariette, the daughter of a wealthy liquor-store owner, spent her days shopping, playing golf and visiting casinos – she and Justin would also go to game lodges on weekends, as well as hosting, and attending, lavish dinner parties. She also attended the local Dutch Reformed Church.

She and Justin made friends easily, and they became particularly close to one couple – Ria and Tienie Wolmarans. The women took classes together in cake decoration and making porcelain dolls. The foursome would take one of their BMWs and travel around the countryside, past the poverty, and out to the stunning Botswanan scenery.

But in 1995, everything changed. Justin was killed in a car crash. Devastated, Mariette sought solace with someone she was closest to. She and Tienie Wolmarans started an affair, often driving to nearby motels to engage in – as he described it in court – "good sexual intercourse". Their relationship grew stronger as that between Tienie and Ria became strained. They had, in fact, separated briefly in 1993, but only for a short time.

Now, however, the marriage was cracking, and Tienie told Mariette he would divorce Ria and marry her. There were just a few things to sort out. Days turned to weeks and Mariette grew impatient. It was time to take matters into her own hands.

On the evening of 26 June 1996, Ria was at home alone. She had been making a cup of tea. Whether she knew about the affair between her husband and Mariette is not known – certainly there were no signs of forced entry. So, however their relationship stood, Mariette was let in by Ria. Perhaps they chatted, perhaps the tea was for them to share. But at some stage Mariette pulled a 9-millimetre Browning pistol from her handbag and shot Ria Wolmarans twice – once in the stomach and once in the ribs, the tea tray falling to the floor beside her. Her daughter Maryna found her later that night.

The police believed that it was a burglary gone wrong. Botswana was much safer than South Africa, but the white population still remained a potential target for those around without such riches. Three months passed, and no one had been arrested. It looked very much like no one would be. Mariette and Tienie rented a house together soon after. In September, they became secretly engaged. It must have seemed to Tienie that fate had somehow intervened to get him the woman he now loved.

CRIMES OF PASSION

Quite why Mariette had decided to tell her sister-in-law, Judith, that she was in love with Tienie a few days before the murder is a mystery. Judith had never liked her brother's wife. But it seemed incomprehensible that Mariette would have committed murder, so Judith forgot about it.

That was until Mariette did a curious thing – she gave the gun to Judith's husband to look after and told the couple she was off to Pretoria to buy a wedding dress. The love, the gun, the dress – it didn't take Judith long to become suspicious. When her husband went to work the next day, she took the gun to the police.

With Mariette away, the police called Tienie in for questioning. They told him about the gun. He said nervously, "I pray the gun and cartridges don't match." His prayer went unanswered – it was the gun that had killed his wife.

Mariette was arrested and charged with first-degree murder. The Dutch Reformed Church paid for her bail, and she spent the time between arrest and trial at home. Tienie married her during this period and was also questioned as an accomplice, but no evidence could be found.

In court, it was revealed that in June 1996 she had driven to Pietersburg in South Africa and borrowed the gun from a friend. The next day, she smuggled it across the border into Botswana. Then she went to see Ria and killed her in cold blood.

She was found guilty and sentenced to be hanged. According to those close to her, she was sure she would still be released – this was not the sort of world she moved in, one where the worst happens, at least not to her. The case was taken to appeal in 2000, but the judge stood firm. "I have not been able to find one moral extenuating circumstance," he said. "You are not very young, you were not intoxicated and you were not provoked."

On Friday 30 March 2001, the death warrant was read out to Mariette, informing her she would be executed the next day. She was not allowed a last meal or any visitors. Tienie was to have visited her on the Friday, but this was "postponed", he was told, until the following Monday. By then, the body of Mariette Bosch was already buried in an unmarked grave in the prison grounds – the first white woman ever executed in Botswana.

MARY CHANNING – THE MOCK WIFE

Thomas Hardy is known as one of England's greatest writers, and much of his writing was centred around the county of Dorset. He wrote about ordinary people in an extraordinary way – farmers, milkmaids, poultry keepers and publicans – and his stories seldom had happy endings.

But one woman from Dorset captured his imagination and kept appearing in his novels and poems. Her name was Mary Channing, and her fate was as tragic as that of any of his characters.

She was, like many Hardy heroines, a victim of circumstance – the circumstance being that she was a passionate and strong-willed woman at a time when to be so was dangerous. She had, people of the time said, "a sluttish disposition," which often gave way "to vanity, promiscuity and riotous living."

Born wealthy in 1867 to Richard and Elizabeth Brooks, she was soon the bane of her despairing parents' existence. Wishing her to get on in life, they packed her off to Exeter and then London, with the hope that she would start to move in the same high-class circles they did. Instead, she drank and partied, attending dances and going home with strange men, becoming the talk of local gossips, especially as she would often turn up in bars with her "suitors", whom she showered with gifts until she was broke.

Her parents decided there was only one solution – to find Mary a suitable husband, from a good family. Surely their daughter would then return to the straight and narrow. A large dowry was set, to attract young men who may have been put off by Mary's reputation.

Thomas Channing, a grocer of good but not outstanding means, offered his services. On 15 January 1705, having barely met each other, the pair were wed. Hardly pausing to consummate the marriage, 18-year-old Mary partied for two days, only occasionally in the company of her husband. Within three months she had begun a new affair, with a Mr Naile, on whom she spent large amounts of her husband's money, and who replaced her husband in her bed.

How willing Thomas Channing was to allow Mary to take lovers is unclear, but – it seems – he wasn't that keen. Despite the licence she was either given or took, he soon became a hindrance to her, and she hit upon a solution that would prove brutally effective – the introduction of mercury into his rice milk. She did so on 17 April 1705, just after their third month married.

Thomas was violently ill and spent three days vomiting. Clearly a man well-ordered in his habits, he guessed he was being poisoned and took the time to write his will between bouts of throwing up, leaving everything to his father. He died on 21 April, and the post-mortem immediately revealed traces of the mercury.

By then Mary was long gone, hiding first elsewhere in Dorset and then with friends in neighbouring Somerset. Her husband's death was national news, and once it was revealed that she had purchased mercury shortly before his death, there could be no doubt that Mary Channing was the killer. Afraid of being tried as accessories, her Somerset friends turned her in.

The jury deliberated for less than an hour. Mary Channing, despite pleading her innocence, was found guilty of murdering her husband and sentenced to death. At that time a death sentence was carried out by one of the grislier means of execution – Mary would be burned at the stake. It was then that Mary revealed that there was an extra circumstance to be considered – she "pleaded the belly", which meant she was pregnant. By law, she could not be killed until the baby was born.

This meant that the execution had to be delayed. Her parents used the delay to petition Queen Anne for their daughter to be spared. A further petition was sent to the judge in the case. Both were ignored.

In her spartan cell, Mary continued to plead her innocence. On 19 December she gave birth to a son – whether he was the son of Thomas Channing will never be known. Mary had him baptized and nursed him until 8 March 1706, when she was brought again before the courts and asked if there was any new evidence she could offer that would stay her execution. She could offer none. Her son was taken from her, and she was told to prepare for death.

Maumbury Rings, on the outskirts of Dorchester, is a Neolithic earthwork constructed over 5,000 years ago. The Romans used it as an amphitheatre, and in the seventeenth-century English Civil War, it was used as a gun emplacement. Now, a stake was to be placed at the centre of it, and a teenage Mary Channing burned to death.

It is said nearly 10,000 people turned out to watch. She was carried through the crowd and tied to the stake by her neck. Wood was piled at her feet. And at five o'clock – it is said the late hour allowed the sheriff to finish his afternoon tea – she was set alight.

It was 200 years later that Hardy took up his pen. Women trapped by circumstance and the herd mentality of village folk were large themes in all of his work, and Mary won his sympathy. He didn't feel she had been given a fair trial, and the presence of so many at the execution revolted him. His poem, "The Mock Wife", exonerates the heroine, who is based on Mary, and in it she and her husband share a last kiss, with her husband expressing his gratitude and love.

No one knows what happened to Mary's son. His name was changed for his own protection, and he is lost to history. Not lost, though, is Mary, who lives on in Hardy's work and in the history of Dorset, as a true example of what was once said by the historian Laurel Thatcher Ulrich: "Well-behaved women seldom make history."

SUSAN WRIGHT – 193 SHOTS OF MADNESS

On 13 January 2003, 26-year-old Susan Wright tied her husband, 34-year-old Jeff, to their bed in Houston, Texas. She later told police he was on a cocaine binge at the time – a regular occurrence. Also regular, she told them, was the physical abuse he put her through. He had already beaten her that night, she said, and she had taken the chance to restrain him to prevent further violence.

No one knows when she decided to go to the kitchen and get two knives – she herself said she couldn't really remember. Nor did she remember the first time she drove the knife into him, or where. But she did remember going into a frenzy, and by the time she was done she had stabbed her husband 193 times – including 41 times to his face, 46 to his chest and seven in his pubic region. The tip of one knife broke off and was left embedded in his skull. It was the end of a terrible and tragic relationship.

They had met in 1997 when she was 21 and he was 29. At the time she was working in a topless bar, which the prosecutors would later use against her. She soon fell pregnant, and they were married in 1998, a month before the baby was due.

Two years later, they had a second child, a daughter to go with their son.

By then, according to Susan, Jeff was regularly attacking her and had begun to be violent towards the children. Several times she showed bruises to her mother, who would later testify in her defence. His drug-taking was constant, and Susan said she never felt safe.

That January night, according to Susan, Jeff had already beaten their four-year-old son. He then raped his wife and threatened to kill her, before passing out. She saw her opportunity and tied him to the bed. The years of abuse would end there and then.

Afterwards, she tried to cover up her crime. She tied him on a dolly and wheeled him outside, burying him in a hole he himself had dug to install a fountain. The next day, unable to remove the bloodstains with bleach, she repainted the bedroom. She also filed a domestic-abuse report so she could obtain a restraining order against her husband, and therefore explain his absence.

But the strain was too great. On 18 January, five days after the killing, she phoned her attorney, Neal Davis, and asked him to come to her house. He did, and she told him she had killed her husband and buried him in the yard. On 24 January, she turned herself in to the police.

At the trial she told the judge and jury about the abuse she had suffered – but the judge and jury didn't believe her. The prosecution managed to portray her as a loose woman – the topless bar was held up as an example – and money-hungry. Jeff had taken out $200,000 of life insurance shortly before his death. She was, the press said, "a monster" – the 193 stab wounds were proof of that. On 3 March 2004, she was sentenced to 25 years in prison.

Was it self-defence? Susan's story became more plausible five years later. During an appeal hearing, a new witness, Misty McMichael, took the stand. She was an ex-fiancée of Jeff Wright. She had broken off their relationship because of his violent behaviour towards her. This evidence, plus an assessment that said that Susan's "counsel rendered ineffective assistance during the punishment phase of trial" didn't overturn the original conviction, but her sentence was reduced to 20 years.

She was paroled in 2020. Eight years earlier, a film had been made of the crime, called *Blue-Eyed Butcher*. But the French title might be better: *193 coups de folie* – "193 Shots of Madness".

BRYNN HARTMAN – PROFESSIONAL JEALOUSY

After Brynn Hartman shot her husband, she drove straight to a friend's house and confessed to the killing. But the friend, Ron Douglas, seeing she was intoxicated, didn't believe her. Everyone knew that their relationship was a tempestuous one, and many people knew about her struggles with addiction, but this didn't make sense. After all, they were no ordinary couple. She had been an actor and model. And he was one of the most famous comic actors in the world. But when Douglas got back to Brynn's house at 6.20 a.m., there could be no doubt – Phil Hartman had been shot three times, and their two children were crying in their beds.

Phil Hartman had found fame in the 1980s on *Pee-wee's Big Adventure* (1985) and then *Saturday Night Live*. By 1998, he was one of the biggest names in comedy – starring in *NewsRadio* and voicing multiple characters on *The Simpsons*. Described by people in the industry as a low-key, regular guy, he was hugely sought after for his comic skills and no-fuss attitude.

But for all his success and calm demeanour, Hartman had a more sombre side. Never comfortable with the spotlight, his growing fame made him increasingly reclusive and liable to stay "in character" between shots. His second marriage to real-estate agent Lisa Jarvis had just ended, with Jarvis telling *People* magazine that offscreen Hartman "would disappear emotionally... he'd be in his own world. That passivity made you crazy."

It was on a blind date that he met Brynn Omdahl, an aspiring actor and model. The attraction was instant. They were married a year later, and had two children. To the outside world it looked like a perfect marriage.

But Brynn had her own demons. Having moved to LA to become a star, her failure had driven her to addiction, particularly cocaine and alcohol. She was also addicted to the antidepressant Zoloft. As her husband became more successful – he even tried to get her roles – her lack of success drove her to bouts of anger and depression, and on several occasions Phil removed the children from the home when she was being verbally or physically abusive.

She was not only jealous of his success, but of his other relationships – friends, family and exes. When Phil's former wife, Lisa Jarvis, sent him a card of congratulations on the birth of their first child, Brynn wrote her a savage letter, including a death threat. "The gist of it," said Jarvis, "was, 'Don't ever get near me or my family, or I will hurt you.'"

On 27 May, Brynn had been out for dinner. When she returned, the couple had an argument, and Phil went to bed. At around 2 a.m., Brynn entered the bedroom with a .38 Smith & Wesson and shot her husband multiple times in the head and chest as he slept in bed. He died instantly.

An hour later, after she had drunk more alcohol, she called Ron Douglas, telling him Phil was gone for the evening and had left her a note saying he'd be back later. He told her to get some sleep. Twenty minutes later she turned up at his house, hysterical and smelling of booze. She collapsed on his floor and Douglas carried her to the bathroom to throw up, fearing she had taken an overdose.

Even then, she was still holding the gun, and she told Douglas she had shot her husband. Douglas miscounted the number of bullets left in the gun and didn't believe her. It was then that they returned to the Hartman house, and Douglas made his horrific discovery. At 6.20 a.m. he called 911.

As the police raced to the scene, family friends arrived to help remove the children, Sean and Birgen, then aged nine and six. Brynn locked herself in the bedroom, next to her husband. Before the children left, they heard what Sean would describe in court as what sounded like a door being slammed again and again. It was, in fact, gunshots. Brynn had shot herself with the same gun she used to kill her husband. Toxicology tests later showed that she had a blood-alcohol level of approximately 12 per cent, as well as evidence of the presence of cocaine and antidepressants.

The news caused shock around the world. That night's rehearsals of *The Simpsons* were cancelled, and Hartman's characters were immediately dropped. *NewsRadio* had his character die of a heart attack between series, producing an episode in which the other characters reminisced about his life.

But as tributes flowed in, more and more stories about the couple's tempestuous relationship circulated, and Brynn's addictions became public knowledge. The children were subsequently raised by Brynn's sister.

The couple had, on multiple occasions, begun divorce proceedings, but remained together because of the children.

CRIMES OF PASSION

And now their names will be linked forever. Not only due to the crime, but because of the stipulations of their wills. Both were cremated at Forest Lawn Memorial Parks and Mortuaries, Glendale, California, and their ashes scattered together at the nearby Emerald Bay.

Chillingly, both are commemorated at Greenwood Cemetery in Minnesota. They share a single headstone, showing his birth date "Sept. 24, 1948", and hers "Apr. 11, 1958". And their death date – "May 28, 1998" – only a few hours apart. And now together forever.

FLORENCE RANSOM – THE MYSTERIOUS LONG BROWN PACKAGE

The shotgun, she told her brother Frederick, was to shoot rabbits. Of course, she would need some training. Would he oblige? It was 8 July 1940, during rationing for World War Two, and Florence Ransom's brother, who was an experienced shooter, was more than happy to teach his sister how to aim and fire. She was good at it. And her brother was happy to lend her the gun.

Ransom had spent the last six years as the lover of a married man, Walter Fisher. Walter and his wife, Dorothy, had an unconventional marriage, particularly for the 1930s. Soon after their wedding, Dorothy had taken a Danish lover, and Walter had given his okay, continuing to live with his wife, first in the London suburb of Richmond, and then in Twickenham.

In 1934, Walter met Florence Ransom, and they too became lovers. Dorothy was aware of this, and also gave her okay. The couple organized their marriage around their lovers, and for a long time it worked.

CRIMES OF PASSION

But in 1938, they decided to split amicably – Walter moved in with Ransom at her farm in Bicester, Oxfordshire, and also bought a house for Dorothy in Crittenden, Kent. Dorothy moved there with their teenage daughter, Freda. Walter also paid for a maid. After the Blitz started, he would visit regularly to check his ex-wife and daughter were safe. It appeared everything had worked out to everyone's satisfaction. But jealousy is a funny thing, and it seems that Walter's regular visits to Dorothy started to gnaw away at Ransom.

The day after visiting her brother, Ransom was seen on the 8.56 a.m. train from Bicester, carrying a long brown package. She was later seen on another train, between Tonbridge and Crittenden.

It is believed that when she arrived at Dorothy's house in Crittenden, she was first approached by Freda, then aged 20. She may have told her the same story about shooting rabbits, as she and Freda walked off together through an orchard attached to the property. When they came to the end of the orchard, Freda must have been in front of Ransom, as she was shot at close range in the back.

Dorothy heard the shot and came running. What she saw must have terrified her, as she turned and started to run away from Ransom. Ransom chased her and shot her in the back as well, two bullets killing her instantly. Ransom then walked back to Freda and shot her twice more, to make sure she was dead.

She then went into the cottage, where the maid, Charlotte Saunders, was making tea. She may have let Ransom, who was well known to her, in the door, before gathering her tea tray to take out to the garden. The tray was later found upturned next to her body – Ransom had shot her in the head.

The bodies weren't discovered until 6.45 that evening. A local, John Leury, was making a delivery, and halfway up the drive he came across Dorothy's body. The police found the other bodies soon after. Suspicion immediately fell on Walter Fisher and Florence Ransom.

Walter had an alibi. Ransom claimed she had been at the farm all day, but she was unaware that at least three locals had seen her near Dorothy's house on the day of the killing. In one case, after the time of the murder, the witness reported seeing the woman running, a strange sight, and that she kept almost dropping a brown paper package.

A taxi driver also identified her. A woman had left a train at Tonbridge at 4.15 p.m., wanting to get to Sevenoaks. The driver pointed out that it was quicker if she went back to the station and got the next train. She jumped out of the taxi and caught the 4.25 train. The woman was, again, carrying a brown package.

The police visited Ransom's brother and found the shotgun, which was positively identified as the murder weapon, tying Ransom to the killing. And finally, a white glove was found at the scene – exactly matching one at Ransom's house. She had taken it off to remove the spent cartridges from the gun.

Florence Ransom appeared at the Old Bailey, London's highest court, and was charged with three murders. The defence pleaded insanity – she could remember nothing of that day, it was a complete blank. The jury was not convinced. They found her guilty, and the judge had no option but to sentence her to death. Ransom collapsed as the verdict was read out, screaming that she was innocent.

It was her last coherent statement – if she hadn't been insane at the time of the murder, the verdict made her so. At the appeal hearing she spent the whole time waving her arms and muttering to herself. Her death sentence was revoked, and she was committed to Broadmoor Asylum, where she disappears from history.

NANCY KISSEL – THE MILKSHAKE MURDERER

It was a case that rocked Hong Kong, and it became known as the Milkshake Murder. When 39-year-old Nancy Kissel decided to murder her husband, 40-year-old investment banker Robert Peter Kissel, her weapon of choice was... a strawberry milkshake. But as she was to find out, it wasn't enough to finish him off. More traditional methods would have to be employed.

The pair had met and married in 1989 and relocated to Hong Kong in 1997, where their three children attended Hong Kong International School. Robert was an extremely successful banker, employed by Goldman Sachs to run their Asian concerns. Soon after, he was headhunted by Merrill Lynch, to head its "distressed assets" operations. The couple lived well, with a US$20,000-a-month ocean-view apartment, and to the outsider it seemed a perfect marriage – perhaps even to an insider like Robert.

What Robert didn't know was that Nancy had begun an affair in 2003 on a visit to their American home, located in Vermont. Michael Del Priore was a twice-married electrical repairman who had rewired the Kissel home. The affair was torrid, and when Nancy returned, they exchanged long and frequent telephone calls.

Robert became suspicious and hired a private detective, Frank Shea, to spy on his wife. He also installed spyware on her computer to track her movements and communications. It soon became evident to him that his wife was seeing someone else. According to Nancy, he initiated divorce proceedings and was determined to take custody of the children.

And so, Nancy decided to kill her husband. On 2 November 2003, she laced a strawberry milkshake with sedatives, including Stilnox, and gave it to her six-year-old daughter to deliver to Robert before she took the children to school. When she got back, her husband was unconscious but not dead. So, she took an eight-pound metal statuette and bludgeoned him to death.

Next, she rolled his body up in a carpet and placed it in the storeroom of the apartment complex. Then she went and collected her kids.

When Robert failed to turn up for work – a workaholic, it was inconceivable that he would do so without letting his employer know – the police issued a missing-person alert, and Nancy was immediately questioned as to his whereabouts. When she failed to provide adequate answers or explain why she had not reported him missing, a search of the apartment complex was ordered, and Robert's body was found. Nancy immediately confessed.

The trial began in June 2005, some 18 months after the murder. Under cross-examination, Nancy claimed that she had killed Robert in self-defence – he was abusive towards her, had raped her over a five-year period, and his highly strung, workaholic personality had led him to self-medicate with cocaine and alcohol. When he had proposed divorce, they had argued and he had sexually assaulted her, before swinging at her with a baseball bat. That was when, she said, she had grabbed the statuette and bludgeoned him to death, although she had no memory of delivering the five blows that killed him.

As for the milkshake, she claimed she had not poisoned it. Once, back in the States, she had added a little Stilnox to a drink of Robert's to try and calm him down, with little success. She had tried the same thing in Hong Kong, but when she saw it left sediment on the bottom of the glass, she tipped it away. Perhaps she had not rinsed the glass properly before it was reused for the milkshake?

The jury didn't believe her. After a trial that lasted for 65 days, they took only eight hours to find her guilty. She was sentenced to life in prison. Various appeals failed, including an attempt to claim diminished responsibility due to provocation. But at that appeal, the prosecution noted that she had been having an affair with Michael Del Priore and argued that she had considered running away with him. Might not the US$18 million she would have inherited on the death of Robert been handy if she did? She remains in a maximum-security prison in Hong Kong, where she continues to plead her innocence.

FATAL AMBITIONS

It's the classic format of a good story. A character wants something – money, a job, fame, freedom. Something stands in their way – a rival, an enemy, poverty, family. The character must overcome this barrier to get the thing they want. They do, and then they live happily ever after.

What motivates someone to kill? Hatred of another, yes, but not always. The goal lies beyond the person sent to their grave. The victim is just a barrier, and their removal is, in a way, nothing personal. They could have been anyone who just happened to get in the way.

As we will see, money is quite often the driving force of murder – this whole book could have been about women poisoning their husbands to get at their inheritance and, especially, life insurance. It sometimes feels as if it would be easier to count the late nineteenth-century men who weren't poisoned by their wives than those who were. Arsenic seems to have been everywhere, and the woman of the house, doing all of the shopping and chores, tended to have easiest access.

But you don't just get life-insurance payouts on husbands, you do on your kids too, and several women did their sums and doubled their money. Arsenic may not be present in flypaper these days, but it turns out that in the US in the 1980s, there was cyanide in fish-tank cleaner. This is the sort of information you can obtain if you borrow lots of books on poisoning, as Stella Nickel did before her husband mysteriously died.

If poisoning is too complicated, or lacks the thrill of being there when a victim dies, there is still bludgeoning. Easier if the victims are the elderly, as Dorothea Puente's were. They may not have life insurance, but if they are getting benefit checks, they can be cashed for years.

Or strap a bomb on someone and make them rob a bank. Of course, if they don't get it right, the bomb goes off. Marjorie Diehl-Armstrong thought of this. A cunning plan, but, as it turns out, not an entirely successful one.

And so, whether their ambition is money, fame or, as in the case of Sachiko Eto, to become a god, as we will see, the sky is the limit in terms of the ways in which they went about reaching their goals.

DOROTHEA PUENTE – THE DEATH HOUSE LANDLADY

How do you make a lot of money? Some people hope for one gigantic payday, when they will win the lottery or inherit millions. But others are happy to do things gradually – a little bit here and there – until they are comfortably off and, perhaps later, wealthy.

It's the same if you murder for money – sometimes you hit the jackpot. But one woman was happy to gradually build her finances, one social security cheque at a time. And in doing so, Dorothea Puente became one of the most notorious serial killers in US history.

Born in 1929, she was orphaned at six, both her abusive alcoholic parents having died within two years of each other. In 1960 she was jailed twice, once for working in a brothel, once for vagrancy. She was married and divorced twice, both times to violent men, one 19 years her junior. In her mid-30s, she started working in elderly care. She soon realized there was money to be made.

Her method was simple. She tended to focus on the vulnerable – the homeless, those with disabilities and the elderly. She would combine being their landlady with being their carers, first in an apartment, then in a boarding house. Initially, this just meant stealing from them. She forged their benefits cheques and cashed them in. She was caught forging a cheque in 1978, was sentenced to five years' probation and banned from running any boarding house in the future.

Four years later in 1982 – after a third brief marriage – she was arrested again, this time for administering drugs to her tenants in the upstairs apartment she rented out. She was also charged with 34 counts of grand theft and forgery. This time she was sent to jail and served five years in a California State Prison, where a psychologist diagnosed her with schizophrenia.

It was later revealed that one of her tenants, 61-year-old Ruth Munroe, had been found dead in the apartment in 1981. She had died of an overdose of codeine and Tylenol. Puente claimed Munroe had been suffering from depression as her husband was terminally ill. Munroe's death was eventually declared a suicide.

As soon as Puente was released from prison, she started an illegal boarding house in Sacramento. By now she had refined her methods. She would still drug her tenants and take their cheques – but why the hassle of doing that week after week, when one large dose would send them to their deaths? And, as she worked out, if the death wasn't reported, the cheques would keep coming in...

It was a plan she had hatched while inside, and during that time she had started corresponding with Everson Theodore Gillmouth, a 77-year-old retiree from Oregon. On her release in September 1985, she was picked up by Gillmouth, and Puente wrote to his sister shortly after to let her know the pair were to be married that November. Soon after, she employed a handyman, Ismael Carrasco Florez, and asked him to build a 6-foot by 30-inch by 30-inch storage box, with Gillmouth's truck as part-payment.

The day after Florez delivered the box, he returned for payment to find the box nailed shut and weighing, he estimated, 300 pounds. Puente convinced him to help her take it to a storage facility, but in the end they dumped it beside a river. On 1 January 1986, a fisherman found a body in the river, but it was not until 1998 that it was identified as Gillmouth – he had not been reported missing, and his benefit cheques had continued to be signed and cashed.

In the autumn of 1986, 78-year-old Betty Mae Palmer took up residence with Puente and started having her cheques mailed there. In October, another 78-year-old, Leona Carpenter, moved in, following a flurazepam overdose. Given Carpenter's health condition, Puente was somehow able to convince authorities to give her power of attorney over Carpenter. Both Palmer and Carpenter then went missing, although no one was aware of it, as their cheques continued to be cashed.

Again and again, the pattern repeated throughout 1987. James Gallop, 62, recovering from a malignant tumour; Eugene Gamel, 58, who died of a drug overdose shortly after moving in; Vera Faye Martin, 61, who moved in and, two weeks later, failed to contact her daughter on her birthday for the first time and never contacted her again; Dorothy Miller, 65, who went missing soon after arrival – Puente later hired a carpet cleaner to remove a large stain from what had been her room.

In February 1988, Alvaro "Bert" Gonzales Montoya, 51, arrived and ceased attending his appointments with social workers in August – Puente said he had gone to Mexico and then convinced a man who worked in her yard to tell social security that he had driven Montoya to Utah. Finally, there was Benjamin Fink, 55, who moved in on 9 March. His brother visited him weekly for six weeks, but then Fink went missing. A foul smell was coming from his room; Puente told other tenants it was a blocked pipe. Then she ordered 12 bags of concrete and had a hole dug in the yard and the concrete poured in.

It was the disappearance of Montoya that first raised suspicions. Montoya was developmentally disabled and had schizophrenia, and when he failed to turn up to his appointments, alarms were raised. The story of him going to Mexico or Utah didn't make sense, given his condition. In November 1988, police obtained a warrant to search Puente's boarding house for clues, although they did not at that point regard her as a suspect. It was only when they saw a recently disturbed patch of ground and the hole filled with concrete that the investigation pivoted. They ordered the ground be dug up, and what they discovered was horrifying.

Betty Mae Palmer's dismembered body was found – her head, hands and lower legs were missing, and toxicology results revealed she had died of an overdose. Nearby was the body of Leona Carpenter, also dead of an overdose. Under a gazebo they found James Gallop, and under a metal shed, Vera Faye Martin. Dorothy Miller was found under a concrete slab next to some rose bushes.

Montoya was also buried in the yard, as was Fink, wrapped in a plastic knotted bedspread and secured with duct tape. He was covered with blue absorbent pads to absorb odours – this detail would lead them to connect Puente with the dead man discovered in the river.

In all, nine bodies were dug up. All of them had been poisoned with a combination of prescription drugs. And each of them had continued to receive social security payments. Puente was now on the run.

She didn't get far. On 16 November, she was spotted in a bar in Los Angeles and arrested at her hotel soon after. Returned to Sacramento, she was immediately charged with the killing of Montoya, and then in March 1989, with nine counts of murder. She pleaded not guilty.

The trial lasted six months, and the jury took almost two weeks to reach a verdict. Puente was found guilty of three murders – Benjamin Fink, Leona Carpenter and Dorothy Miller – with the other six charges ending in deadlock, as some members of the jury regarded the evidence as circumstantial. Spared a death sentence, on 10 December 1993, she was sentenced to two life sentences without the possibility of parole.

She continued to protest her innocence until her death in 2011, but she was happy to be called a serial killer on one particular occasion – in 1988 she began corresponding with journalist Shane Bugbee and the pair collaborated on a book of 50 recipes together. Its title? *Cooking with a Serial Killer.*

SARA ALDRETE – THE GODMOTHER

They called her *La Madrina* – "The Godmother". Standing over six feet tall, Sara María Aldrete Villareal would have been an imposing figure even if she hadn't become involved in one of the bloodiest cults in human history. She was officially charged with 16 deaths, but the number of murders she committed is generally thought to be closer to 30. And these were no simple killings, they were ritualistic murders of a horrifying nature.

She was born in Mexico in 1964, attended school across the border in Texas and was known to be a good student. Tall and athletic, on her graduation she seemed destined to transfer to university to study physical education. Then she met Adolfo Constanzo.

Born in Florida to a Cuban immigrant mother, Constanzo had been an altar boy before a childhood encounter with voodoo captured his imagination. As a teenager he experimented with a Cuban religion called Palo, which involved animal sacrifice. As an adult he moved to Mexico City and styled himself as a sorcerer, casting good-luck spells for drug dealers and hitmen. He and his new-found followers continued to experiment with

FATAL AMBITIONS

animals – chickens and goats at first, later zebras, snakes and lion cubs.

Among his clients were the powerful Calzada family, whose growing success Constanzo felt was down to his magic. He demanded a share of their business. They refused. Shortly after, seven members of the family went missing. When the bodies were found, their fingers, toes, ears, and even brains and spines were missing. Constanzo had crossed over from animal sacrifice to human.

On 30 July 1987, Aldrete was driving near her home in Matamoros on the Mexican border when a Mercedes cut her up. The driver stopped, got out and apologized profusely, introducing himself as Adolfo Constanzo. What Aldrete didn't know until later was that this "accident" was nothing of the sort. Constanzo knew her then boyfriend, Gilberto Sosa, who was associated with the high-profile Hernandez family.

The connection between Aldrete and Constanzo was instant. He soon introduced her to magic and the dark arts and stunned her by predicting her break-up with Sosa using Tarot cards. Briefly they were lovers, but Constanzo preferred men, and instead their bond would be played out in more sinister ways. Constanzo had started a cult, known as *Los Narcosatánicos* – "The Narcosatanists", and Aldrete would be his second in command. He was *El Padrino*, "The Godfather", and she was *La Madrina* – "The Godmother".

Initially, their murders were strictly business – they took out members of drug cartels, shooting them in order to grab territory and take profits. But they soon grew dissatisfied, and the murders became more violent and ritualistic.

Setting up a headquarters 20 miles outside Matamoros in 1988, their first sacrificial victim was Raul Paz Esquivel, a cross-dresser and former lover of a cult member. Esquivel's remains were dumped in the street. Soon after, another man was tortured to death – presumably by Aldrete and Constanzo – in order to secure the safe release of a Hernandez family member and his son. The pair were released, and Aldrete and Constanzo claimed credit.

The killing spree continued. According to their version of Palo, in order for a sacrifice to be effective, the greater the pain and mutilation the better. The demons smiled more on those who had suffered before death. "They must die screaming" was the rule.

Their ranch headquarters also held drugs that the Narcosatanists had "earned" through their work – mostly cocaine and marijuana. It was 800 kilograms of marijuana that led to their fatal mistake. Aiming to smuggle it over the border, Constanzo believed a particularly strong spell was needed to guarantee safe shipment. They needed someone with a "good superior brain". He said he wanted someone he could use, someone who would scream.

Aldrete helped find and kidnap the victim, Mark J. Kilroy, a University of Texas student on spring break. Whereas earlier victims had been the sort who could be "disappeared" without much fuss from the police, Kilroy was different. He was affluent and popular, with political connections, and his abduction became world news. Not that it helped Kilroy; he was killed with a machete before the cult realized the net was closing in.

Killing one last victim – Aldrete's former boyfriend, Gilberto Sosa – the cult fled the ranch. When police arrived, they were shocked to find a shrine and the butchered remains of 15 victims, human hair, teeth, brains and skulls. They tracked the killers down to another hideout in Mexico City. A shoot-out on 6 May 1989 ended with the death of Constanzo, shot by one of his followers on his own orders. Aldrete was arrested and charged with 16 murders. She was sentenced to 62 years in jail.

Was that the end of the Narcosatanists? One cult member was explicit when they were arrested. Constanzo may have died but, he said, "The godfather will not be dead for long."

MARY ANN COTTON – PASSING THROUGH NATURE TO ETERNITY

On 18 June 1583, Richard Martin of London invented a new type of financial arrangement. Martin paid 13 merchants £30 each, to receive £400 in return if a man named William Gybbons died within a year. It is not recorded what state of health Gybbons was in, why Martin was so interested, nor indeed if Gybbons got through the 12 months unscathed. What we do know is that Martin's new arrangement was to become a mainstay of capitalism; a highly recommended piece of individual economic planning; and in turn would lead to some of the bloodiest murders in human history. Richard Martin had invented life insurance.

History does not record the first murder committed in order to take advantage of Martin's idea, but given how keen humans seem to be to kill each other, and how keen they seem to be to make a buck, it is unlikely that much time passed between 1583 and the first "transaction". As a playwright of the time, William Shakespeare put it, "If money go before, all ways do lie open."

FATAL AMBITIONS

We can never know if Mary Ann Cotton was familiar with the works of Shakespeare, but we do know that she was very familiar with the concept of life insurance. Britain's first serial killer didn't make a profit from all 21 or so lives she took – she could sometimes bring herself to do it for free – but she did all right, that's for sure.

Born Mary Ann Robson in 1832, in Durham, in the north of England, she was first married at 20, having worked as both a nurse and a dressmaker. Her husband, William Mowbray, was a labourer, and over the next decade they produced eight or nine children.

A prudent man, William decided at some point to make sure his wife and dwindling number of children were looked after in the event of his death. He took out a life-insurance policy in 1864. He did so just in time – soon after doing so, he too died of gastric fever, as did two of the remaining children. Mary Ann received £35, about half a year's wages.

She left the remaining child, Isabella, with her mother, and moved to Sunderland, where she started working at Sunderland Infirmary. There she met George Ward, who was a patient at the hospital. They married on 28 August 1865. His health seemed to improve a little, but then he started to deteriorate, and on 20 October 1866 he died, and his death certificate records typhoid. Though he had been unwell, doctors were surprised at the sudden onset of his final illness. Mary Ann had taken out insurance and now collected.

Husband number three was James Robinson, a shipbuilder in Sunderland who had employed her as a housekeeper. Robinson's wife had recently died, and Mary Ann was soon offering more than housekeeping, bringing him comfort after his infant son died – of gastric fever – and falling pregnant to him. At the same time, her own mother had a health crisis, suffering from hepatitis, and Mary Ann moved back to look after her. Her mother then started to suffer from stomach pains and died, so Mary Ann took Isabella back to live with her, James Robinson and his two other children, Elizabeth and James Jnr. A few weeks later all three children were dead, and Mary Ann received £5 for Isabella.

The grieving parents married in August 1867, and their daughter Margaret was born that November. She died the following February. A son, George, followed in 1869. It was then that James Robinson discovered Mary Ann had run up debts and stolen money. He threw her out, and kept George – one might surmise that George had a lucky escape.

Destitute, she was living on the streets. A friend, Margaret, introduced her to her brother, Frederick Cotton, a recent widower living in the Newcastle suburb of Walbottle. Margaret was helping to look after his son Charles.

Despite her straitened circumstances, Mary Ann showed she had lost none of her charms, and the pair were married on 17 September 1870 – Margaret did not attend as she had died of a mysterious stomach ailment in March, soon after introducing Mary Ann to her brother. That Mary Ann was still married to James Robinson was not mentioned to her new husband. A son, Robert, was born in early 1871 – her twelfth child – and in December her new husband Frederick died. Mary Ann collected the insurance. Another lover, Joseph Nattrass, moved in, they had a child, and then Joseph died. As did the child.

She had one child left – Frederick Cotton's son, Charles Edward. When a parish official, Thomas Riley, asked her to help nurse an ailing local woman, Mary Ann asked him if Charles could be taken from her and put in a workhouse.

FATAL AMBITIONS

When she was told no, she is reported to have said that she wouldn't be troubled long, as he would go like the rest of the Cottons. He did.

Riley was suspicious, especially when Mary Ann went first to the insurance offices instead of the doctor. Charles Edward was exhumed. His young body was filled with arsenic.

Mary Ann was arrested and charged with one count of murder. She was held in custody and gave birth to one last child. The trial was over quickly – despite her defence counsel's valiant attempts to argue that Charles had inhaled arsenic from wallpaper. Since her arrest, more and more details of her life had emerged, and the wallpaper defence was fooling nobody.

On 24 March 1873, she was hanged at Durham County Prison. The hangman, William Calcraft, was an experienced one, who ended the lives of approximately 450 murderers at the gallows. He was known, in special cases and for the entertainment of the crowd, to make the rope too short to break the neck as the body fell, which meant the victim died of strangulation instead, a much more terrible death. It seems he regarded Mary Ann Cotton as a special case.

No one knows exactly how many of her victims were waiting for her on the other side – at least 21 – but perhaps if Richard Martin hadn't been so interested in the health of William Gybbons, they wouldn't have got there so soon.

SANTE KIMES – MUMMY AND CLYDE

She met with the wife of Richard Nixon. She met with then vice-president Gerald Ford. She impersonated Elizabeth Taylor. Before she was sentenced, she and her son were interviewed on *Larry King Live* and *60 Minutes*. After sentencing, the judge called her "one of the most evil individuals" she had encountered in her time on the bench.

Sante Kimes was good at what she did – a brilliant con artist whose fraudulent schemes netted her huge amounts of money. But she was more than that – she was also a cold-blooded killer, although we will never know how many lives she took.

Sante was born in Oklahoma City in 1934, the third of four children. Her life fell to pieces when her father left and her mother, Mary, turned to prostitution. Caught and convicted, Mary was forced to give up her children, and Sante was adopted by Edwin and Mary Chambers as "Sandra Chambers". A cheerleader at school, she turned to petty theft, and by the time she was 27 she had already been married and divorced twice.

She met her third husband soon after – motel tycoon Kenneth Kimes, and they had a son, Kenneth Kimes Jnr. Kimes Snr was wealthy, and the family had homes in Las Vegas, California,

FATAL AMBITIONS

Hawaii and the Bahamas. The couple talked their way into the White House twice, meeting Patricia Nixon and Ford.

But still Sante carried on with her petty thefts. She also added arson to her repertoire, burning down her husband's properties for insurance money. Kenneth Kimes' fortune dwindled as he paid legal fees to cover his wife's crimes.

The couple were arrested in 1985, for slavery – Sante would find young illegal immigrants and force them to work for her by threatening to turn them over to the authorities. Kenneth was left virtually bankrupt, as well as being sentenced to five years in prison for violating federal anti-slavery laws. He took a plea bargain, agreeing to complete an alcohol treatment program. Sante refused and was jailed until 1989, which is when things got darker.

In September 1990, Sante paid her lawyer, Elmer Holmgren, to burn down her husband's house in Honolulu. Insurance investigators questioned Holmgren, who admitted his involvement. Soon after, his own office, containing documents that would implicate Sante, burned down. Then in August 1991, Holmgren disappeared, after telling his family he was going to Costa Rica – with Kenneth and Sante. He was never seen again.

Kenneth Snr died in 1994 of a brain aneurysm. A year later, in November 1995, an associate of the Kimes family, Mary Jacqueline Levitz, heiress to the Levitz Furniture fortune, went missing. A relative who called at her house found the front door open. The bedroom was covered in blood, and there were torn off fingernails on the floor. Although Sante was never charged with her murder, similarities to the cases she was found guilty of make it likely she was involved.

By now Sante was working with her son, Kenneth Jnr, and the pair would later be dubbed "Mummy and Clyde" by the press. Some of those who knew them suspected an incestuous relationship – certainly they were always together, and neither one ever had other partners. As one person who investigated the case put it: "Kenneth didn't have friends. No one was good enough for him. He grew up with her as a dominating force."

The first confirmed victim of the Kimes pair was 63-year-old David Kazdin. Sante had forged his signature to obtain a $280,000 loan. When he discovered the forgery, Sante ordered her son to kill him. Kenneth shot Kazdin in the back of the head.

Soon after, Sante hatched a scheme to steal the identity of 82-year-old socialite Irene Silverman and take ownership of her $7.7-million New York townhouse. Kenneth Jnr moved into an apartment in the mansion, using an alias, and then he and Sante recorded Silverman's phone calls and built up an elaborate plan for fraudulently taking over her life and possessions. Soon after, Silverman left her home and was never seen again.

However, what neither Kenneth nor Sante knew was that they were already under investigation. On 14 March, Kazdin's body had been found in a dumpster near Los Angeles airport. Documents owned by Kazdin implicated them in his killing. Police were also able to trace the handgun used to kill Kazdin – it had been sold to Kenneth Kimes Jnr.

Mother and son were arrested on 5 July at the New York Hilton in a sting organized by the FBI and NYPD. In their stolen car were Silverman's keys and tape recordings of her phone calls, as well as loaded guns, plastic handcuffs, a "date rape drug", an empty stun-gun box and $30,000 in cash. They also had a signed deed, transferring ownership of Silverman's mansion to a shell company in their name.

FATAL AMBITIONS

The pair were charged in New York with the murder of Silverman as well as 117 additional charges such as robbery, grand larceny, burglary and forgery. During the trial, the judge continually had to censure Sante for attempting to influence the jury by using her prison calls to speak to journalists instead of lawyers, in the hope that the jurors would read her version in interviews. Sante herself compared proceedings to the Salem witch trials, crying out that prosecutors were "murdering the constitution" by trying an innocent woman and her son.

Sante and Kenneth Jnr were sentenced to 120 and 124 years in prison, respectively. They were then to be transferred to California to stand trial for the murder of David Kazdin.

Shortly before being transported, Kenneth took reporter Maria Zone hostage by holding a pen to her throat and threatening to kill her. He demanded that he and his mother not be extradited. After four hours, he briefly moved the pen and was leapt on by authorities. The pair were extradited in 2001 and stood trial in 2004.

During the trial, Kenneth struck a plea deal with prosecutors – he would tell them everything if he and his mother would be spared the death penalty. He then testified in the trial against his mother.

He admitted to killing Kazdin and described how his mother had used a stun gun on Silverman, and how he had made sure she was dead by strangling her. The pair had then thrown her body into a dumpster in New Jersey.

He also told them about a third victim, Syed Bilal Ahmed, a 46-year-old banker who was in charge of Sante's accounts in the Bahamas. Kenneth said the pair had drugged Ahmed, then drowned him in a bathtub, before dumping his body. Under questioning, Sante denied all knowledge of this crime, arguing that Kenneth had made it up in order to escape the death penalty. Neither was ever charged.

But they didn't need to be. Both were given life imprisonment on top of their earlier sentences. Sante died in prison on 19 May 2014, still claiming that the whole thing had been a stitch-up. Irene Silverman's body has never been found.

ROSEMARY NDLOVU – COP TURNED KILLER

"Meeting Rosemary was the biggest surprise. You know, she is charming; she is warm." So said the director Valen'tino Mathibela after she interviewed Rosemary Ndlovu for a documentary she was making about what Rosemary had done, called *Rosemary's Hitlist*. And what she had done was horrific.

Ndlovu had killed six members of her family, including her sister and her live-in partner and father of her child, in order to live off their life-insurance policies. She had been convicted and sentenced to six concurrent life terms for the killings, plus an added 30 years for fraud, incitement to commit murder and the attempted murder of her own mother.

But Mathibela didn't think she did it just for the money. "Money was not enough of a reason. Murder alone is already chilling, but this was the destruction of a family by one of their own."

She admitted being fascinated by the case: "Because it's unbelievable. It's a cop! Killing her family!" Her other surprising talent, she said, was an "ability to distance herself from the responsibility of the crimes and her mastery of the alibi."

Perhaps she need not have been surprised – charm has been one of the main weapons of the serial killer for all of their bloody history.

Rosemary Ndlovu was born in 1978 in Bushbuckridge in Mpumalanga, South Africa. When she graduated from high school, she joined the South African Police Service (SAPS), one of the first Black women to enter the force after the end of apartheid. She rose to the rank of sergeant, and became a popular and well-respected member of the force.

There was only one real blot on her copybook: she liked to gamble, and on more than one occasion she failed to come to work in order to avoid loan sharks from whom she'd borrowed money to feed her addiction.

Mathibela might be right that her murders weren't just about money, but it certainly motivated her first kill in March 2012. Her cousin, Witness Madala Homu, was found beaten to death. While it was obviously a case of murder, South Africa is one of the more violent places on earth, and little was done in the way of investigation – it was just another dead body in a township where such things were not uncommon. Ndlovu pocketed 131,000 rand in insurance, around £6,000 at current rates.

Her sister Audrey was found dead a year later. She had been poisoned and strangled, but even though it happened at Ndlovu's house, she was not considered a suspect. The police suspected a male, possibly a robber – that seemed more likely than an upstanding female police officer. Again, she claimed the insurance money, almost five times as much as she had received on the death of her cousin. That same month, her niece, Zanele Motha, died, again having been beaten, and again there was an insurance payout.

FATAL AMBITIONS

It is hard to imagine what Ndlovu was thinking as she carried out her crimes. These were no quick or easy deaths – her victims must have fought back against their family member. Was her need for money – or her pleasure in killing – so extreme that she didn't even pause for a moment?

In October 2015, she killed her live-in boyfriend, Maurice Mabasa, who was also the father of her child. He suffered 76 stab wounds. Again, there was a life-insurance payout, as there was in April 2017, when her nephew Mayeni Mashaba, who had been seen with her the day before he was killed, was also found dead.

By now, surely, Ndlovu must have thought things were looking suspicious, but perhaps having killed five relatives and cashed in on them, she thought she was unstoppable. So killing her dead sister's son, Brilliant Mashego, a few days after taking out an insurance policy on him, was just another day's work.

However, if she did think she was unstoppable, she was about to be proved wrong. Unbeknown to her, a secret police operation was beginning to close in. Two undercover policemen, posing as hitmen, took a recording of her attempting to enlist them to carry out another insurance hit – bigger than any of the others. She wanted them to burn down her sister Joyce's house, to kill her – and her five children. This would have doubled her list of murders, and presumably doubled her insurance earnings. Six dead, six lots of insurance – the hitmen could take a generous cut. She was arrested the same day and sentenced after a short trial to a life sentence for every murder she committed.

But it doesn't seem that prison has changed her. She has since been charged with attempting to organize the murder of the husband of Nomsa Mudau, a friend from the police force, as well as the murder of the two male officers who brought her to justice, Sergeant Keshi Mabunda and Colonel Nthipe Boloka. She had no insurance money to gain from the death of any of them – in this case it would seem, she just wanted them dead.

NANNIE DOSS – THE GIGGLING GRANNY

Some called her "The Black Widow", the female equivalent of Bluebeard – a person who marries and then kills their spouse, or in most cases, spouses. But mostly she was known as the Giggling Granny, because even in custody, and even after confessing to killing four of her five husbands, her mother, her sister, her grandson and her mother-in-law, well, she did still like a laugh, Nannie Doss.

She was born in Alabama in 1905, and at the age of nine she banged her head on a metal bar when a train stopped suddenly. All her life she would suffer from headaches, and when she was tried, she cheerfully blamed the injury for her abnormal behaviour, such as – it would seem – killing people. As a teenager she started reading romance novels and, in her words, fell in love with love.

At 16 she was married for the first time, to Charley Braggs, whom she had only known for a few months. They had four children between 1921 and 1927, but Doss found living with her mother-in-law intolerable. Two of the children died in mysterious circumstances. When Braggs went to work in the morning they were happily playing; when he returned, they were dead, apparently having suffered convulsions not long after breakfast.

They were both insured, and the insurers paid out. But the marriage couldn't survive the death of the children, and they divorced in 1928. Braggs took his older daughter, Melvina, with him and left a newborn, Florine, with his ex-wife and his mother. He would later claim he left because he was frightened of Doss.

Braggs' mother died soon after, and Doss got married again, to Robert Franklin Harrelson, whom she had met through a Lonely Hearts column. She soon found out that Harrelson was an alcoholic and had a criminal record for assault. But the marriage would last for 16 years, during which time Doss was presented with her first grandchild. Her daughter, Melvina, who had stayed in touch, gave birth to a baby boy, Robert Lee Haynes, followed by a granddaughter two years later.

It was when they were staying with Doss that Melvina thought she saw her mother press a hatpin into her daughter's head. When Doss announced moments later that the baby was dead, she was holding the pin, but doctors found no evidence of a wound. Two years later, Melvina's son Robert died mysteriously under Nannie's care on 7 July 1945. Two months later, Doss collected $500 for an insurance policy she had taken out on the boy.

Soon after, on 15 September, Harrelson came home drunk after celebrating the end of World War Two. Doss – who later claimed Harrelson had raped her – laced his whisky with rat poison and he died in agony the same night. With the life-insurance money from Harrelson's death, Doss bought a plot of land and a house near Jacksonville.

FATAL AMBITIONS

Returning to the Lonely Hearts column, she soon met her third husband, Arlie Lanning. They married three days after they met, and he too soon proved to be an alcoholic. He was also a womanizer. Their marriage lasted only two years, before Lanning died of what was later diagnosed as heart failure. Their house also burned down, and Nannie Doss collected the insurance money.

Soon after, in 1953, Doss's mother fell ill and she went to nurse her. Days later she was dead. Doss went to share her grief with her two sisters, and while she was with them, both died, each with the same mysterious symptoms of convulsions and stomach cramps.

Again, Doss hit the Lonely Hearts column, this time walking down the aisle with Richard L. Morton. His mother came to live with the happy couple. Morton died a year later, on 19 May 1953, his mother having mysteriously predeceased him, despite her robust health.

Less than a month later, she married her final husband, Samuel Doss of Tulsa, Oklahoma. A few months later he was admitted to hospital with what was diagnosed as a severe digestive tract infection. A week later he was dead. An autopsy revealed that he had in his system "enough arsenic to kill 20 men". The two insurance policies Doss attempted to claim made the perpetrator obvious.

Finally arrested, she proved a jovial figure, chuckling as she recounted the grisly details of her murders. Money was not the motivating factor, she told the police. It was boredom. None of her husbands had lived up to the characters she read about in romance novels, none of her family made her laugh. She had been, she told her interrogators, searching for the perfect mate, the real romance of life.

MARJORIE DIEHL-ARMSTRONG – EVIL GENIUS?

It was described as "one of the most complicated and bizarre crimes in the annals of the FBI", an organization that has seen its fair share of complicated and bizarre crimes.

When pizza-delivery man Brian Wells entered the PNC Bank at Summit Towne Center on Peach Street, Erie, Pennsylvania, at 2.30 p.m. on 28 August 2003, he was sucking a lollipop. He waited in line and on reaching the counter produced a handgun and slipped the teller a note. The note stated that he had a bomb attached to a collar around his neck, and it would go off in 15 minutes. The teller was to hand over $250,000. The teller explained to Wells that he could not access the vault so quickly, all he could do in that time was hand over all of the cash held behind the counter, which turned out to be $8,702. Wells accepted and left the bank swinging the bag of money and his gun "like Charlie Chaplin", according to one witness. At 2.38 p.m., a 911 call informed police that a man had robbed the bank, and shortly afterwards he was arrested.

Wells explained to the officers that the bomb was set in such a way that any attempt to remove it would detonate it. Police concentrated at first on securing the area to ensure no one would be harmed. Wells was left isolated, kneeling surrounded by police cars. At 3.04 p.m. the bomb squad was called.

Meanwhile, police searching his car had found a chilling letter. Addressed to the "Bomb Hostage", the letter was a series of instructions, the first being to rob the bank, and then a series of "scavenger hunt" tasks to be completed in order to delay the bomb's detonation. On completion of the last task, the bomb would be defused. Scrawled at the bottom was "ACT NOW, THINK LATER OR YOU WILL DIE!"

The bomb squad was three minutes away when the collar bomb went off, killing Wells instantly and covering the street and the police cars in blood. In order to remove the bomb as evidence, the police had to sever Wells' head from his body.

A month later, the police received a call from William Rothstein, a handyman and robotics teacher from Erie, who was also part of a group called "Fractured Intellectuals", for intelligent people who did not fit in well with society. Rothstein told them that the body of a man, James Roden, was hidden in a freezer at his house. On finding the body, Rothstein told them that he had been killed by Roden's girlfriend in a dispute over money, and that she had given Rothstein $2,000 to help her clean the crime scene and hide the body. Her name was Marjorie Diehl-Armstrong, and this would not be her first trial for murder.

Born in 1949, Diehl-Armstrong was precociously intelligent, top of the class and a lover of poetry, often quoting from Sylvia Plath or John Milton. Diagnosed bipolar, she told a reporter she saw this as a positive – some of the greatest artists and writers who ever lived were bipolar, listing Lincoln, Churchill, Teddy Roosevelt, Van Gogh, Beethoven and Hemingway as examples.

In 1984, she had shot her boyfriend Robert Thomas six times but had been acquitted on grounds of self-defence. Rothstein was also an ex-boyfriend – they had dated in the late 1960s and early 1970s.

Diehl-Armstrong was arrested for Roden's murder. She pleaded guilty, but in view of her mental state, the offence was downgraded. During questioning and the trial, she was an erratic speaker – prosecutors had more trouble stopping her talking than getting her to. She was sentenced to between seven and twenty years in prison, depending on behaviour.

But had she killed Roden in a dispute about money? Gradually her own words and a number of pieces of evidence started to build the story that she had killed Roden to stop him going to the police about a planned robbery that involved a bomb placed around the neck of a hostage…

Evidence suggested that Diehl-Armstrong, Rothstein and another man, Kenneth Barnes, had planned the robbery, possibly with the assistance of a fourth conspirator, Floyd Stockton. The $250,000 was, in fact, to pay Barnes to carry out another crime – Diehl-Armstrong wanted to pay him to kill her estranged father, so she could claim her inheritance.

According to prosecutors, Rothstein, who died before the case was tried, had built the bomb, but Diehl-Armstrong and Barnes had been the masterminds behind the plan – a subsequent Netflix documentary would take its name from the idea that Diehl-Armstrong was an *Evil Genius*.

It is understood they met Brian Wells through a prostitute he was familiar with who, in turn, bought crack off Kenneth Barnes.

A major question was how much Wells himself knew about the plan. In some versions, he was led to believe that the bomb would be fake, in order to scare the bank teller and give him a way of pleading his innocence if caught. It seems certain that he knew about the robbery in advance, as he was later revealed to have spoken about it a month before it occurred. It is possible he was only told the bomb was real after it was placed on him, or that he still believed it was fake, which might explain his calm demeanour in the bank. What is known is that he was instructed to claim three Black men had placed it on him.

Kenneth Barnes was sentenced to 45 years in prison, with his sentence later halved in a plea deal to testify against Diehl-Armstrong. In 2008, she was found mentally incompetent to stand trial but remained in custody for the killing of Roden. In 2009, she was judged competent, and a new trial date was set for 2010 to be held in Erie – the only place Diehl-Armstrong had ever lived. She tried to have the trial moved, given the notoriety of the case, but this was refused.

On 1 November 2010, she was convicted of armed bank robbery, conspiracy to commit armed bank robbery and of using a destructive device in a crime, and sentenced to life imprisonment, to be served concurrently with her sentence for the murder of James Roden.

She continued to plead her innocence, saying that it was a political thing, a cover-up and that she would fight it until her dying breath, which she said she hoped would not come too soon. It came on 4 April 2017.

BELLE GUNNESS – HELL'S BELLE

Belle Gunness had, as anyone in town could tell you, already lived a life of great hardship. And now this – on 28 April 1908, her farmstead burned down, with her inside. A terrible end to a life of terrible events, so they said.

She had been married twice, but both of her husbands had died, one of a cerebral haemorrhage, one when a meat grinder fell from a shelf onto his head. And then there were her children. The two babies from her first marriage had died from inflammation of the large intestine, while the daughter of her second marriage had died in unknown circumstances.

Belle had been born Brynhild Paulsdatter Størseth in Norway in 1859, the youngest of eight children. Emigrating to America in 1881 to join her sister, she changed her name and found work first as a domestic servant and then in a butcher's shop, where her physical strength and dexterity with a knife marked her out. It is said she weighed 200 pounds (90 kilograms), and one man who helped her move house saw her lift a 300-pound (135-kilogram) piano by herself.

She soon met and married Mads Sorensen and they opened a candy store. It burned down not long after the pair had found themselves in financial difficulty. Fortunately, the couple were insured and received a large payout, as they did on the deaths of their two babies, although some were surprised by the latter, as no one remembered Belle being pregnant.

The death of her first husband would have shaken a lesser woman, but fortunately it happened on the very day that two life-insurance policies overlapped, and she was able to claim on both and pocket the $5,000, using it to buy the farmhouse.

With Peter Gunness, her second husband, she had a child that died, and then she had to suffer losing her husband too, via falling meat grinder. Belle pocketed another $3,000 after a long investigation by both the insurers and the police.

Then, six years later, the fire. Inside the farmhouse, the charred body of a headless woman was found, as well as the bones of three children. It was known that Belle had been placing marriage ads in Chicago newspapers, and that at least two men had answered them. Had she had more children?

But neither of the men had been seen at the farmhouse by anyone. When their families were contacted, it turned out both were missing. There was also a third man, Andrew Helgelien, who had answered Belle's personal ad, which read, "Comely widow who owns a large farm in one of the finest districts in La Porte County, Indiana, desires to make the acquaintance of a gentleman equally well provided, with view of joining fortunes." It added that "Triflers need not apply."

Helgelien's brother Asle went with the police to investigate. A search of the farmhouse found a small depression near a pig pen. Digging into them, they found "two hands, two feet and one head". Asle recognized his brother.

There were, in fact, dozens of shallow graves around the property, each containing sacks with torsos and hands, and arms hacked from the shoulders down. There were also masses of human bones with dripping flesh. All the corpses had received the same treatment – the arms removed completely, the legs cut off at the knees, and the heads removed and smashed in. "The bones had been crushed on the ends, as though they had been... struck with hammers after they were dismembered... Quicklime had been scattered over the faces and stuffed in the ears," the police report read.

In all, 11 complete bodies were found, spread throughout the yard. Most could be identified, and some were incomplete, meaning there may have been more. Some say the police simply stopped counting as the task became more and more grisly. One body they did find was that of Belle's foster daughter, Jennie Olsen. Could this be linked to when Olsen had allegedly told her friends at school (referring to Peter Gunness), "My mama killed my papa. She hit him with a meat cleaver and he died. Don't tell a soul."

And the headless woman in the burned farmhouse? Was it Belle? The newspapers weren't convinced. It seemed too neat a death for "Hell's Belle" or the "Indiana Ogress" as they were now calling her. And why was the head missing?

There is a final page in the case file of Belle Gunness. In 1931, a woman named Esther Carson was arrested in Los Angeles for poisoning a Norwegian-American man and attempting to steal his money. She looked very similar to Belle, only 23 years older than in 1908, when the farmhouse had burned down.

Unfortunately, she died of tuberculosis while awaiting trial.

DELFINA AND MARÍA DE JESÚS GONZÁLEZ VALENZUELA – LAS POQUIANCHIS

"The food didn't agree with them," said 55-year-old Delfina González Valenzuela when she and her 40-year-old sister María de Jesús were arrested for murder in January 1964. If that were true, it seems then that their food didn't agree with a lot of people – a search of their brothel had revealed 91 corpses – 80 women and 11 men, plus a large but unquantifiable number of babies and foetuses. Rancho El Ángel was already known as the "brothel from hell", but perhaps not even hell had seen the horrors that were present in San Pancho, Mexico.

The authorities had been tipped off by three mothers who arrived weeping at the police station in León. Each had a teenage daughter missing, and a young girl had turned up in their village and told them about a nearby ranch where girls were being held captive. Storming the ranch, the police found the three girls and 16 others being held captive. The 19 girls were dirty and emaciated, some of them chained to walls.

But worse was to follow. One of the officers stepped on a piece of newly dug earth, his foot going through the surface and hitting something soft. It turned out to be a human arm. Police had stumbled on not just a brothel but a killing field – or as they put it, "a concentration camp for white slaves".

Delfina and María de Jesús were two of four sisters born in poverty in El Salto de Juanacatlán. Their father was violent and known to have shot another man during an argument. If his girls dressed inappropriately, or wore too much make-up, he would lock them away at the local jail.

When they reached adulthood, the women opened a bar, then quickly diversified into prostitution, opening a series of clandestine brothels. They bought another bar in Lagos, Jalisco from a man nicknamed "El Poquianchi". The nickname was passed on to the sisters, who were now called "Las Poquianchis", a nickname with no real meaning. They were to give it one.

They began recruiting girls from the slums, promising them jobs as maids or waitresses. Instead, the girls found themselves living in cells at the brothels and put to work. They were never allowed to leave the ranch. The police search found a number of instruments of torture, for use both by clients and the sisters.

If a girl fell pregnant, the foetus was disposed of, usually by being buried. Girls who became ill, got an STD or were left incapacitated by an abortion were either locked in their cells to starve to death or beaten to death by the sisters, or by other girls who were forced to do so as an example. Others were doused in kerosene and set alight.

Worst of all, according to the girls who survived and gave evidence, was a device called the *cama real*, meaning "royal bed". Girls were placed on a narrow board and wrapped in barbed wire, so any movement would cause agony. They would be left there for hours or even days at a time as punishment for any mistake.

The sisters were also happy to kill their clientele if they arrived with a fat wallet. For them, death at least came quickly: they were generally shot by the sisters or one of the security guards. The 11 male bodies found at the ranch were thought to be just a small selection.

When the arm was found, the police immediately arrested the two sisters. The other two sisters, Carmen and Luisa, who ran brothels elsewhere but coordinated their activities with Las Poquianchis, were arrested shortly after. As they were taken from the ranch, an angry mob of villagers formed, demanding to be allowed to lynch the women.

The 19 girls remaining pointed out places around the ranch where they knew bodies were buried, but in reality there were few spots where the police didn't find another victim. As some of the bodies had been cut up, the task of working out how many had died was almost impossible. The final figure of 91 was an educated guess.

At the trial, more stories emerged of the cruel and unusual activities of Las Poquianchis. They were accused of satanism and making the girls perform sex acts with animals in occult rituals. There were also accusations of rape and bribery – it was highly unlikely, the judge said, that all local authorities had been unaware of what was going on.

The women were sentenced to 40 years in prison each, the maximum under Mexican law at the time. Delfina, always seen as the leader, suffered a complete mental breakdown in jail, spending her entire time believing she would be tortured and killed. She did, in fact, die in an accident, struck from above by a falling bucket of cement on 17 October 1968. One of the other two sisters, Luisa, also died in jail of unknown causes – her corpse had been eaten away by rats before an autopsy could be performed. María de Jesús served her time and then disappeared from history.

But the story was not over. In 2002, the land around where Rancho El Ángel once stood was being cleared for a new housing development, and workers were horrified to discover the skeletons of another 20 murdered men and women. How many more still remain to be found, victims of the notorious Las Poquianchis?

LYDA SOUTHARD – LADY BLUEBEARD

For a long time, it seemed that bad luck followed Lyda Southard. Born Lyda Keller in Missouri in 1892, she married for the first time at the age of 19 – a local boy by the name of Robert Dooley. Their families had known each other forever, and when Lyda moved to Twin Falls in Idaho, Robert followed her and proposed. With an eye to their future security, life-insurance policies were taken out on both Robert and his brother Edward – $1,000 to the surviving brother and the same to Lyda.

Two years later, after the birth of their first child, Lorraine, in 1913, tragedy struck. On 9 August 1915, Edward, healthy until then, suddenly died of suspected typhoid. The grieving Robert and Lyda received $1,000 each. The day following Edward's death, a new policy was taken out on the lives of the husband and wife, for $2,000 to go to the survivor. The survivor quickly turned out to be Lyda, as Robert was also struck down with typhoid a month after his brother and died, leaving his widow in possession of all his belongings, the life-insurance payout and their daughter – who was also insured.

And who also died. Six weeks after the death of Robert, Lorraine, according to Lyda, drank contaminated water and followed her father and uncle to their graves.

After a period of mourning, lasting some 18 months, Lyda married again in 1917, taking as her beau a waiter in her favourite Twin Falls restaurant, which she had begun frequenting soon after the triple tragedy. She made sure her new husband, William McHaffle, was as prudent with money as her first husband and arranged for them both to take out life insurance as soon as they were wed, this time for $5,000. William had a three-year-old daughter, who passed away soon after their wedding.

Alas, William himself was no more resilient than Robert had been and died of influenza a year later. To Lyda's chagrin, during her mourning period she became aware that William had failed to make a payment that was due, and the life-insurance policy was invalid.

Perhaps her disappointment in William enabled her to recover from her sorrow at another dead husband more quickly, as a mere six months later, in March 1919, she again got married, this time to Harlen C. Lewis – an automobile salesman from Billings, Montana. But he too, it seems, was a man of a fragile constitution – he died four months after their marriage, of gastroenteritis. Fortunately he was insured, and so Lyda was not left empty-handed.

A fourth husband followed – Edward F. Meyer, married August 2020, dead September 2020. He had, according to his death certificate, also died of typhoid. Unfortunately for Lyda, insurers had refused to allow her a policy; her awful luck made her a bad risk.

Watching all of this from afar was a chemist in Twin Falls – a relative of her first husband, Robert. Earl Dooley had begun to suspect that Lyda's run of dying husbands and children may not have been down to the bad luck people were ascribing to it. Dooley decided to consult Twin Falls Deputy Sheriff Virgil Ormsby. Ormsby first ascertained from the Idaho State Life Insurance Company of Boise that Lyda had collected around $10,000 of insurance money, which would be close to $200,000 today.

Ormsby then ordered that Robert, Edward and little Lorraine be exhumed. An autopsy revealed the presence of arsenic in their bodies, in lethal doses. This does not happen naturally. As a homemaker at that time, Lyda would have had access to arsenic – it was, for instance, used in flypaper. A warrant was issued for her arrest.

By now, 1921, she was in Honolulu and had married again – this time a naval officer, Paul Southard. Southard refused to take out an insurance policy – if he died the government would support her for life. Whether this would have been enough reward for Lyda was never tested – she was arrested in May, despite the protestations of her devoted husband.

The trial was a sensation – the press nicknamed her Lady Bluebeard, after the tale of the husband who kept murdering his wives. She continued to claim that all of those who had died around her had done so of natural causes, while admitting it was curious that all of them had fatal intestinal ailments.

Of the 150 witnesses for and against, the most sensational was a Montana shopkeeper, who recognized Lyda as a woman who had bought vast quantities of flypaper from her. As the prosecution noted, when boiled, the poison on flypaper that killed the flies would come off into the liquid. That poison was arsenic. The jury deliberated for 23 hours before finding her guilty. She was sentenced to life imprisonment.

However, it was not the end of her amorous adventures. Paul stuck by her until 1928, when he finally divorced her. In 1931, she somehow convinced a prison guard to lend her a saw, and she cut through the bars of her cell, escaping into the arms of ex-convict David Minton, who offered to marry her. She wasn't interested and fled to Denver with an assumed name, where she met and married Harry Whitlock, who had a nine-year-old son, Benny. She took out life insurance on Harry immediately.

But then something remarkable happened. It is understood that Benny adored Lyda, and so when she snuck back to Kansas to visit her sick mother, she wrote to Harry giving him her real name, knowing that he could claim the $50 reward offered for her capture, which he could use to start a savings account for Benny. Lyda always thought ahead when it came to money.

Back in prison she remained a model prisoner and was pardoned in 1943. As soon as she was released, she met and married her seventh husband, Hal Shaw. His horrified friends and relations pressured him to divorce her. He didn't get a chance – he disappeared soon after they were wed...

Lyda herself died in 1958, back in Twin Falls, Idaho, where it had all begun.

MARQUISE DE BRINVILLIERS – THE MARQUISE OF DARKNESS

They say that practice makes perfect. For many murderers who choose poison as their weapon, the first murder is also the first time they have used poison. It makes the whole thing a risky business. Too much or too little – especially too little – can have disastrous consequences. In a perfect world for a murderer, a few test runs could only be a help.

When Marie-Madeleine-Marguérite d'Aubray, the Marquise de Brinvilliers, decided with her lover, army captain Godin de Sainte-Croix, to poison her father Antoine Dreux d'Aubray and two of her brothers, Antoine d'Aubray and François d'Aubray, in order to inherit their estates, she was prepared to put in the hours needed to become an expert.

Born in 1630, she had married the Marquis de Brinvilliers in 1651 and was described as "a pretty and much-courted little woman, with a fascinating air of childlike innocence". When the marquis was stationed in Normandy, she took the opportunity to do what any pretty and much-courted marquise would do – she started an affair with a handsome cavalry officer, Godin de Sainte-Croix. Scandalized, her father had Sainte-Croix arrested, and he spent a year in jail. On his release, he returned to his lover, and they decided to kill her family and run away together.

They enlisted the help of a chemist, Christopher Glaser, who produced poisons for them of various strengths. The marquise, with all her connections, saw a way to get just the right thing. Poor people often sought her charity, and she was known to visit hospitals as part of her courtly duties. Why not try the poison out on the poor and infirm? Surly no one would miss them?

Estimates vary on exactly how many test cases the Marquise de Brinvilliers experimented on, but at her trial, a number around 50 was agreed by most parties. Whether there were others who survived we don't know. Presumably as time passed, survival became less and less likely.

Finally satisfied with her efforts, in 1666 she did indeed poison her father, who died on 10 September. Soon after, she poisoned both her brothers. Unfortunately for the young lovers, Sainte-Croix himself suddenly died. Even more unfortunately, among his possessions was a box of letters between himself and the marquise, detailing their crimes.

The marquise fled to England and managed to stay on the run for two years, helped no doubt by her aristocratic connections. But it was in Belgium that the law caught up with her. Among her possessions was a letter titled "My Confessions", which detailed the various crimes she had committed. Arrested, she attempted to commit suicide several times as she was taken back to Paris, but was unsuccessful. She stood trial in 1676. The French aristocracy followed the trial with huge enthusiasm, gripped by one of their own facing the death sentence. When it was pronounced, the court was filled with fainting women.

It was not to be a gentle death. As part of the sentence, the marquise was condemned to receiving the "water cure" before being taken to the place of execution. This involved being forced to drink 16 pints of water poured into her mouth with a funnel. She was then denied confession and taken to the Place de Grève, where a huge crowd had gathered. There the executioner shaved her head, set her on her knees and raised a sword above her neck. He paused a moment and then chopped her head off. The crowd could then stay around and watch as they burned the body of the woman who had come to be known as the Marquise of Darkness.

MARIAM SOULAKIOTIS – MOTHER RASPUTIN

Sometimes killers come from the least likely places – even a convent! Born in 1883 in Greece, Mariam Soulakiotis was a devoted follower of Archbishop Matthew Karpathakis of Vresthena. When he built a new convent and monastery, she departed from her family home and took holy orders. In the course of her life, Soulakiotis rose to be the Abbess and Mother Superior of the Panagia Pefkovounogiatrissa Monastery and Convent. Also in the course of her life, she killed at least 177 women.

She was known for her devotion and for taking care of the day-to-day running of the place, while Matthew was occupied with ascetic monastic practices, such as spending time in isolation chambers, tying heavy chains to his body and engaging in 40-day fasts. For 11 years she served under him, and on his death in 1950, she assumed total control. By then she was already a murderer.

Her method was simple. She would encourage wealthy women to join the convent, to pray, serve and save their soul. Once inside they would find themselves isolated, away from friends and family. They lived in small cells, with little outside contact.

FATAL AMBITIONS

Often, she lured women to the convent with the promise of a miracle cure for tuberculosis. The high altitude of the monastery would work its miracles on them, she said, as would their sparse diets and closeness to God.

Once they were there, she would torture them until they donated their fortunes to the church, then in most cases kill them. This was either done directly or through making them take part in awful modes of devotion – sleep and food deprivation or corporal punishments, as well as blackmail and beatings. No doctors were allowed to visit to tend the sick, only to sign death certificates.

It is believed around 150 women died a slow death this way, each of them signing over their fortunes in the hope of a tuberculosis cure that never came, or for the salvation of their soul.

The first time Soulakiotis came under police suspicion was in 1949. The daughter of a wealthy woman who had willed all her property to the monastery made an anonymous complaint, stating that her mother would not have done so voluntarily. Soon after, the father of a missing 18-year-old girl also contacted police, claiming his daughter had been lured into the convent, donating $10,000 for the salvation of her soul.

On 4 December 1950, 85 police officers raided the convent. They rescued 46 children and a large number of elderly women, all of them – children and women – naked and malnourished, who were being held in a basement. They also found the remains of the 177 dead, buried in the grounds. The press dubbed Soulakiotis "Mother Rasputin", after the Mad Monk who had served the last Tsar of Russia, Nicholas II.

But hers was a difficult case to prove. Most of the women had arrived voluntarily, and those with tuberculosis had died of natural causes, albeit with added neglect. So, she was initially charged with the illegal export of olive oil to Cyprus, as well as the illegal import of tyres. Then while she was in custody, the police were able to piece together more and more evidence and the charges grew to include murder, fraud, forgery, blackmail and torture.

However, she was only actually charged with seven murders – five women who had been locked in cells and starved to death and two others, Sister Theodote and Sister Maria, who had been beaten to death.

She would always proclaim her innocence, as did many of her followers at the time, and many since, some of whom venerate her as a saint. The charges, she said, were "Satanic fictions". She argued that donating money, undergoing suffering and living in isolation were part of a nun's calling, and that those outside the monastic life are in no position to judge.

The jury didn't agree, and she was sentenced to separate prison terms adding up to 16 years in jail.

She died after 14 years in prison and was buried at the convent, next to Archbishop Matthew. The convent is still open, with lavish grounds.

THE LAINZ ANGELS OF DEATH – PLAYING GOD

Waltraud Wagner was the first one to do it. In 1983, working as a nurse in Ward D at the Lainz General Hospital in Lainz, Vienna, she killed a patient with an overdose of morphine. By some accounts, the patient had asked for the lethal dose and Wagner had been reluctant. But if it was an experiment to see how it felt, Wagner decided it felt good. She felt a rush of adrenaline as she watched the patient die. She later said she enjoyed playing God and deciding whether someone lived or died, all down to her whim.

It was the start of a horrific series of crimes with no real equivalent, not just in Austrian history, but in all history.

This is because, unlike most murders, there wasn't just one killer, or even a couple. The "Lainz Angels of Death", as they came to be known, were four women from Ward D who joined together with one mission – to kill as many people together as they could. And between 1983 and 1989, that was a lot of people.

Wagner was able to recruit two other women straight away – 19-year-old Maria Gruber and 21-year-old Irene Leidolf. Leidolf in particular was to show herself to be just as cruel and evil as Wagner. Finally, they recruited Stephanija Meyer, a Yugoslavian immigrant who, at 43 years old, acted as what they called the "house mother" of the group.

All had difficult lives – Meyer had recently been divorced, Gruber was a teenage single mother, Irene was stuck in an abusive marriage. The environment they worked in was brutal, with very ill patients in overcrowded wards. Wagner offered them a way of taking some control.

Initially their method was the same that Wagner had used in the first place – they injected the patients with drugs and watched them die. Most of the patients were elderly and incapacitated, but not all of them were suffering fatal illnesses. The injection was quick, effective and unlikely to be questioned in a medical setting.

There is some possibility that, as the four were to argue during their trial, they were acting out of a sense of compassion for those who were truly suffering. But things quickly escalated. Soon the four were killing patients who annoyed them, were too needy, soiled their bed, failed to take their medication or even snored too loudly. According to court testimony, if a patient used their buzzers too many times in one night, Wagner would tell the others that it was time for the patient to get a ticket to God. She even kept a to-do list of patients to be killed on a given night, as retribution for previous infractions.

But the rush of giving a lethal injection was beginning to wear off. Wagner and the other Angels decided they needed something more extreme – and more painful. They came up with what they would call the "water cure" – an eerie throwback to the medieval form of torture used on murderers like Marquise de Brinvilliers. At least three of them were required for each kill – one to pinch the nose of the patient, one to hold their tongue down and the last to pour water down their throats. The patient would drown, a brutal and agonizing death, and one that would not seem suspicious – water in the lungs is very common in the elderly.

Worse, the death can be very drawn out. The victim keeps trying to swallow, and if they are in any sort of robust health, they can accidentally keep themselves alive for a long period – or of course the murderer can control the amount of water poured, in order to drag it out.

For five years, the killing continued, with over 50 deaths estimated, and with the water cure their preferred method.

It wasn't until the sixth year that the high number of deaths on their particular ward started to draw some attention. Police and doctors called for an investigation, but the hospital, confident in its staff and, no doubt, wanting to avoid a scandal that even a clean bill of administrative health would cause, refused to undertake one. If the Angels already felt like untouchable gods, this would have reinforced it, and the killings continued – estimates put the tally at another 22.

But as everyone knows, there is one thing that will always topple the gods, and that is hubris. As the saying goes, pride comes before a fall. The four women became increasingly careless about covering their tracks. One night after a shift they went to a bar together and, as they drank, not only boasted about the death of their latest victim, Julia Drupal, but described it to each other in great detail. Sitting at the next table, unnoticed, was a doctor from the hospital.

He went straight to the police, and the police began an investigation that lasted two months. On 7 April 1989, after six years of killing, the four women were arrested.

One by one they confessed their crimes, and one by one they pointed to Wagner as the ringleader, which she did not deny. In fact, she was happy to go through the list of victims – 39 had been positively identified – and describe the exact method she used to kill each one. The police were stunned by her photographic memory and attention to detail. When they asked her how she remembered so clearly, she told them that they would remember something like this too.

How many did they kill? In their confessions, a total of 49 victims were identified, but a number as high as 300 hasn't been ruled out. The hospital was investigated for its failure to act – the death rate in Ward D was six to seven times higher than in any other ward, and the ward had gone through 20,500 ampules of Rohypnol in the six years – an extraordinary amount.

At the trial, each Angel blamed the others and presented themselves as having been coerced, but they all also argued that these were mercy killings of patients who were suffering. The jury didn't believe them. Wagner received a life sentence for 15 murders, Leidolf the same for five. Meyer received 20 years on the lesser charge of manslaughter and being an accessory to murder. Gruber also received a lesser sentence, given her youth.

By Austrian law, all life sentences are reviewed after 15 years, and if the prisoner is no longer held to be a danger to society, they are released. And so, by 2008, all four had been released, causing a scandal in Austria. As one newspaper put it in their front-page headline, "The death angels are getting out!" All four were given new names and identities – and the Angels were freed.

VELMA BARFIELD – DEATH ROW GRANNY

She had not, she claimed, meant to kill them. Instead, the plan was to make them sick, steal their money, then nurse them back to health and repay them. If that was true, she wasn't very good at it. Because all six died, all of them in agony.

Margie Velma Bullard, known as Velma, was born in North Carolina in 1932, the oldest girl in a family of nine children. She claimed her father beat and raped her and her sisters, but this was disputed by other family members. Married to Thomas Burke in 1949 before she was 17, she had two children, and the marriage seemed to be a happy one.

But that changed in 1966 – Burke received head injuries in a car accident, and not being able to work, slipped into alcoholism. Velma herself was suffering from back pain and began taking drugs, and then antidepressants. On 4 April 1969, Velma left the house with the children, leaving Burke in a drunken stupor. When they returned, the house had burned down with Burke inside. The cause of the fire was never identified.

A year later she married Jennings Barfield, whose name she took and kept. He died a year later of heart complications. In deep financial trouble, Velma and her children moved back in with her parents. Her father died soon after of lung cancer. And then things got strange.

Her mother suddenly fell ill, showing symptoms of diarrhoea, vomiting and nausea. She recovered, but soon after, it happened again. She died on 30 December 1974.

In 1975, Velma served three months in prison for writing bad cheques. On her release, she began working in elderly care. Two of her patients, 94-year-old Montgomery Edwards and his 84-year-old wife Dollie suddenly developed similar symptoms to Velma's mother. They too died.

Shortly after, Velma began caring for 76-year-old Record Lee and her husband, John Henry. On 4 June, Henry was suddenly taken ill, again with vomiting and diarrhoea. He died within hours.

In the meantime, Velma had started seeing Rowland Stuart Taylor, a relative of Dollie Edwards, and, unbeknown to him, had begun forging his cheques. He too developed the same symptoms, and on 3 February 1978, he too died. As with all the others who had died, Velma attended his funeral and grieved openly.

However, the death of Taylor was so suspicious that an autopsy was ordered – and in his body the doctor found a large quantity of arsenic. Velma was arrested, and the body of Jennings Barfield was exhumed – it too contained traces of arsenic. Although she initially pleaded her innocence, Velma eventually confessed to the murders, describing how she had put arsenic in Taylor's beer and tea. She also confessed to killing her mother, Montgomery and Dollie Edwards, and John Henry Lee – a total of six victims. She was only tried for the death of Taylor – the death sentence she received covered all her crimes.

FATAL AMBITIONS

And it was in being sentenced to death that she achieved a new type of fame and notoriety. Capital punishment in the US, federally suspended in 1972, had been reinstated in 1976. Velma would be the first woman to be executed since 1962, and the first ever by lethal injection.

Her sentence became a battleground for activists on both sides of the capital punishment debate, and her conversion to Christianity in prison added fuel to the fire of abolitionists. But no appeals – judicial or personal – could save her. On 2 November 1984, she was executed at Central Prison, North Carolina. Her last meal was Cheez Doodles and Coca-Cola and her last request was to be buried near her first husband, Thomas Burke. Velma Barfield's life had finally come full circle but getting there had proved deadly for some.

SACHIKO ETO – THE DRUMSTICK KILLER

There have been many different methods of exorcism over the centuries, including prayers, invocations, the use of symbols and rituals, but perhaps no method of driving out demons is as strange as that of Sachiko Eto.

Until she ran a cult, Sachiko Eto lived a very ordinary life. Born in 1947, she was quiet and unassuming. She graduated from high school with good grades, found a job in cosmetic sales, at which she was quite successful, and married her childhood sweetheart, who was a paint craftsman.

They had one daughter and lived in a nice house along the Abukuma River in the Tōhoku region of Japan. They were happy and settled. Then her husband injured his back. Unable to work, he started drinking and gambling, driving them into debt, and they were forced to sell their home.

Soon after, in an attempt to find a solution, they joined a religious group for those not registered to traditional religions. It taught spiritual faith healing. But the couple were kicked out for using the organization's headquarters without permission. Eto's husband had a mental breakdown and disappeared, never to be seen again...

FATAL AMBITIONS

Eto moved 100 miles north of Tokyo and proclaimed that she was a psychic and healer, that she could drive away demons, and that she was a god.

A growing number of followers came to her, so many that neighbours began complaining about all the cars parked outside and all the chanting. There was also the endless sound of drumsticks on taiko drums all day and night. Little did they know that these drumsticks were also used for a more sinister purpose.

Eto had a unique ritual for driving out demons. She said she had to, "kill the dirty body and purify the soul." This involved the possessed person being beaten by Eto with the drumsticks. Her daughter Yuko helped.

In June 1995, one of her female followers ended up in hospital after one of the beatings. On questioning, she told the hospital her husband was missing. He had also suffered a ritual beating, and she hadn't seen him since. Suspicious, the police decided to pay Eto a visit. What they found shocked them.

On the first floor, wrapped in futon mattresses, they found six corpses – two men and four women. Each had been beaten to death. The bodies were in a state of decomposition, showing the deaths had happened several months earlier. Asked why she had left the bodies there, Eto replied that since the soul was not dead, she left them alone. She believed the souls were hibernating and would rise again, although she wasn't absolutely sure it would be in the same body.

Eto, her daughter and three of her followers – including the woman in hospital – were arrested and charged with murder. During the trial, Eto continued to maintain that she had not intended to kill the victims, and in fact she had not killed them but the "ugly devils" inside them. She said she did it as part of a religious service, and never thought they were going to die. She tried to plead insanity, but that was rejected.

Sachiko Eto was found guilty of murder and sentenced to death, and each of her followers, including her daughter, was sent to prison for life. She was hanged on 17 September 2012, aged 65, becoming the first woman to be executed in Japan in 15 years.

DARK SECRETS

As someone once said, the trick to keeping a secret is not telling anyone. Is there anything better to keep secret than the fact that you have killed someone? You may have to answer that for yourself! But the face that the women in this chapter presented to the world was a very different one from that which they presented in private – probably a good idea, as presenting the face of a cold-blooded killer in public won't earn you many friends.

Often the killer with the dark secret can be a loving wife, a loving mother, a good girl at school, a dutiful daughter, a dedicated employee. They gave to charity, nursed the sick, organized cake stalls. After all, murder is not a full-time job, and even the most prolific killers need other pursuits. But the human conscience is a relentless thing, and often makes its disappointment known. The secret will often out. As Lady Macbeth discovered, washing the blood from your hands can be an impossible task.

That said, a few of the women in this chapter got away with it. Most didn't – but then, we probably haven't heard of most of those who got away with murder. As the director Alfred Hitchcock said when asked if there was any such thing as the perfect murder: "Any one where you don't get caught."

Lizzie Borden did get caught and tried, but was found not guilty and lives on in a nursery rhyme. Perhaps her crime was perfect – she got rid of her enemies, found fame and died a very rich woman. Or perhaps, as the jury found, she didn't actually do it. But then why was she burning her clothes the next day?

For others, their secret was only one not to be shared with the law. At times, when contraception was unavailable, extra mouths to feed could be a burden too far. Baby farming – the practice of giving a child away without registering it, to be disposed of one way or another – could be rife. The mother just needed to know who to ask. If you were in Reading in England in the late nineteenth century, that would have been Amelia Dyer, or in Japan just after World War Two, Miyuki Ishikawa. The baby would be placed in their care, and a blind eye turned to what happened next.

If you needed help getting rid of a husband in the Polish enclave of Chicago in the early twentieth century, your woman would be Tillie Klimek. Just ask. But don't tell the men, especially not the ones in uniform.

So, who knows what secrets are out there, still to be revealed? In 2023, the US hit a record high for unsolved murders, and a record low "clearance rate" – murders that had been solved – of less than 50 per cent.

JUANA BARRAZA – THE OLD LADY KILLER

Her professional wrestling name was "La Dama del Silencio" – The Lady of Silence – a reference, she said, to her shy personality. But she is now better known by the name "La Mataviejitas" – "The Old Lady Killer" – a reference to the victims of one of the most brutal and remorseless serial killers in history.

Born in rural Hidalgo, Mexico, in 1957, she was the daughter of a police officer named Trinidad and a prostitute named Justa. Soon after her birth, Justa left her husband and took up with a man named Refugio Samperio, who would become Barraza's stepfather.

At 12, Barraza was pimped out by her mother for the first time to a man named José Lugo, in exchange, she said, for three beers. Lugo made her pregnant at 13 and 16, both times resulting in a miscarriage. It was not until her mother died that she could escape. She then took up wrestling, among other jobs.

She was married several times and had four children by the age of 38, which was when she turned for the first time to robbery, at first by herself and then with a friend, Araceli Tapia

Martínez. The pair pretended to be nurses in order to enter the houses of the elderly and take their money and possessions. Martínez was in a relationship with a police officer, and the couple took 12,000 pesos of Barraza's money in exchange for not having her arrested. No longer earning money from wrestling, Barraza's financial plight became desperate. She decided to take things a step further.

It was in 2002 that murders of the elderly began to increase in Mexico City. The deaths followed a pattern – the victim allowed the perpetrator into their house, then they were bludgeoned to death and their money stolen. It was the first of these facts that baffled the police – how was the killer, now known in the media as La Mataviejitas, winning the trust of the victims?

There seemed to be a breakthrough when a few witnesses claimed that they had seen a large woman in a red blouse leaving the houses of several victims. The police, noting the force with which the victims had been beaten, assumed that the killer must be a man who dressed as a woman to gain the trust of the victim, and started arresting cross-dressing prostitutes – 49 in total – to no avail.

Adding to the confusion, in three cases, the victim owned a print of an eighteenth-century painting by French artist Jean-Baptiste Greuze, *Boy in a Red Waistcoat*. Was this a vital clue, or pure coincidence? It would turn out that it was in fact the latter, but not until various lines of enquiry had taken up more police time.

In October 2005, there were no killings, leading to speculation that the killer had committed suicide, but in November it all started again. While the early murders had generally been poorer women, by now no one seemed safe.

DARK SECRETS

It was not until January 2006, after four years of investigations, that the police got lucky. Barraza was seen leaving the scene of her latest crime, the murder of Ana María de los Reyes Alfaro. She was dressed as a nurse and carrying a stethoscope, with which it would turn out she had often strangled her victims. At her house, the police found objects that had belonged to the victims, plus a room full of newspaper clippings about the murders – despite the fact that Barraza couldn't read.

No one knows how many elderly women she killed, perhaps not even Barraza herself knew. Fingerprints linked her to ten deaths, and she was charged with 16, but prosecutors believed the true total to be between 40 and 50. Her *modus operandi* was consistent – she would gain access to the house pretending to be a nurse or social worker and offer either a massage or to help in obtaining medicines and subsidies. Sometimes she would strangle her victims, other times she would use wrestling moves on them and then strangle them, then leave with money and trophies of her kill.

In March 2008, she was sentenced to 759 years in prison, and is believed to be using her time in jail productively – working as a fitness instructor, helping inmates build muscle.

MIYUKI ISHIKAWA – THE 103

Her biographical note is by turns mundane and chilling: Miyuki Ishikawa, midwife, real-estate agent and serial killer. No one knows how many children's lives she took. Some say 85, some say 169, but generally 103 seems about right. The post-war years in Japan were a time of great confusion and extreme poverty. Many births were not even registered, either because there was no way to do so properly, or because of the shame the mothers felt. This explains why the true number of children Ishikawa murdered will never be known.

It was in January 1948 that two police officers in Waseda District in Tokyo stumbled on the bodies of five infants. It was obvious to the officers that the children had not died of natural causes – an autopsy soon backed up their suspicions. An investigation was launched, and it led to a maternity home called Kotobuki San'in, and to its director, Miyuki Ishikawa, and her husband, Takeshi.

At Kotobuki they found seven more infants, alive but neglected – two died soon after. But it was when they excavated the site that they encountered the true horror – there were the ashes of 40 dead infants in the maternity home itself, and another 30 in the temple in the grounds. Miyuki and Takeshi, as well as the doctor at the home, Shirō Nakayama, were immediately arrested and charged with murder.

Born in 1897, Miyuki was an experienced midwife, having graduated from the University of Tokyo in 1919. Her maternity home was extremely popular – after the Japanese defeat in World War Two, with abortion being illegal, the number of births skyrocketed. Many of Miyuki's clients were extremely poor and, as Miyuki believed, in no position to care for an infant.

So, she and Takeshi hatched a plan – they would take in infants and allow them to die through neglect. But they would also charge the parents, for a price, they said, lower than the child would cost to raise. Nakayama would sign the death certificates. The killing began, and so brazen was it that a number of midwives employed at the home resigned.

How long it would have continued if not for the accidental discovery of the five dead children is anyone's guess. As it was, on 11 October 1948, Miyuki and Takeshi were found guilty of five "murders by omission" – a failure to act – and sentenced to eight and four years respectively in prison, with Nakayama also receiving four years. The sentences were later halved on appeal.

Why were the sentences so light? The post-war years in Japan were a time of great confusion and extreme poverty. A large section of the public supported the couple, arguing they had been forced into the situation by a failure of government. Miyuki herself argued that it was ultimately the parents who were responsible – this was no place to bring babies into. She was merely providing a service, and in the absence of access to abortion, what else could she do? In fact, in 1949, after she had been tried, abortion – for economic reasons – was made legal in Japan, partly because at the end of 1948 it was revealed that 11 other maternity homes also offered the same service as Miyuki Ishikawa.

And "real-estate agent"? After her release from prison, Miyuki understandably changed her career and sold property in Tokyo, and, they say, she made a fortune doing so.

HILDA NILSSON – THE ANGEL MAKER

When Hilda Nilsson killed herself, what she didn't know was that the very day she did it, the court had commuted her death sentence to life imprisonment. It was no act of mercy. Sweden had decided that all death sentences should be pardoned, and she just happened to be next up. No one ever argued for mercy for Hilda Nilsson. And no tears were shed on 10 August 1917 when she took a linen cloth, attached it to the ceiling of her cell and ended a life that had been full of death.

In the beginning, it was about money. She and her husband Gustaf had huge debts and needed to find a way to make money and pay them. It was a time when having a child outside marriage was a source of huge shame – a woman's life would be ruined. Many were eager to pay someone to fix the problem, and Hilda saw her opportunity. She would take the infants into her care in exchange for money. She was not alone in this – baby farming, as it was called, was not uncommon at the time.

Nor, probably, was she alone in what she did next. Rather than fostering the child as promised, she got rid of them – after all, the last thing the couple needed was another mouth to feed.

Her method was simple: she would put the unwanted baby in a tub of water and place something heavy on top of them. She would then leave the room – it seems she got nothing from watching them die – and return to retrieve the dead body. This she would usually burn, although in some cases – for reasons unknown – she was moved to bury them.

It was, in a way, a low-risk crime. The babies were always unregistered – by definition the mothers didn't want their existence known about, and Hilda certainly wasn't going to tell anyone. The children simply disappeared as though they had never existed.

The one flaw in her plan was if a mother had a change of heart, and one of them did. Blenda Henricsson decided she wanted to contact her baby, maybe even take it back. When Hilda was unable to produce the child, Henricsson contacted the police. A raid on Hilda's house revealed various pieces of incriminating evidence, as well as, of course, an absence of all the babies she had been paid to care for.

Called "The Angel Maker" by the press, she was sentenced to death by guillotine. But Hilda got there first, taking one final life – her own.

TAMARA SAMSONOVA – THE GRANNY RIPPER

It was CCTV footage that was her downfall. What was 68-year-old Tamara Samsonova doing hauling garbage bags out of her St Petersburg apartment block in the middle of the night? Where was the woman she had been acting as a carer for, 79-year-old Valentina Ulanova? And what was in that cooking pot?

For her first 50 years, Tamara Samsonova seems to have lived a blameless life – born in Uzhur in 1947, she attended the Moscow State Linguistic University and then moved to Moscow. There she met and married Alexei Samsonova and started working as a travel agent, a job she held until her retirement. And then it all got odd.

In 2000, her husband disappeared. He had been in good health and was known to be a reliable and methodical man, so his absence from work was suspicious. Fifty-three-year-old Samsonova was taken in for questioning and claimed he had simply left. With nothing to tie her to any foul play, she was released without charge.

She began taking in lodgers, including 44-year-old Sergei Potanin. Neighbours heard a quarrel, and then he was silent. He was never seen again.

But it was the death of Valentina Ulanova that showed police what they already knew but couldn't prove. Ulanova lived near Samsonova, and the two were friends. When Samsonova's apartment was being renovated, Ulanova offered to let her stay at hers in return for being her carer, as her health was not good. For several months the arrangement worked, but neighbours again heard arguments. Ulanova eventually asked Samsonova to leave. This, it seemed, was a mistake.

On 23 July 2015, Samsonova offered to cook Ulanova a final meal before she left, so they could at least finish as friends. She would make Ulanova's favourite dish, Olivier salad. The ingredients are boiled potatoes, carrots, dill pickles, peas, eggs and celery. But Samsonova added an extra one, a drug called phenazepam. Ulanova ate, and Samsonova went home.

And then came back. Just as she had planned, Ulanova had collapsed, lying on the kitchen floor. Investigators don't know if she was alive or dead at this point – but she was definitely dead after what happened next. Samsonova proceeded to dismember Ulanova's corpse.

She had returned with a saw and two knives. First, she removed Ulanova's head, placing it in a cooking pot. Then she sawed the body in half and cut it into smaller pieces. These she placed in several garbage bags – the CCTV footage showed her leaving and returning to the apartment over and over, carrying two bags at a time. She had obviously not brought enough bags, as pieces of Ulanova were still discovered around the apartment by investigators.

Three days later, one of the bags was found, and inside were several limbs, wrapped in a shower curtain. As soon as the body was identified, police went to Ulanova's apartment.

Samsonova opened the door to them – there was still blood and body parts everywhere.

They also searched her own apartment and found a diary. Included in the entries was a reference to a previous tenant, Volodya, whom she said she had killed and cut to pieces in the bathroom with a knife, then put the pieces of his body in plastic bags and thrown them away in different parts of Frunzensky District.

Samsonova was arrested and charged with first-degree murder. As she was placed in the police car, she blew kisses at the police and onlookers. When she was informed she would be held in custody, she let out a yell of celebration, as she believed she would be safe from the "maniac upstairs" who forced her to kill.

Police gradually gathered evidence that she was a suspect in at least 11 deaths, perhaps 14 – as she was only tried once, the notoriously secretive Russian police have never released details. She herself was happy to be sentenced to life imprisonment. She said she had thought 77 times about what should happen, and then decided that she must be in prison.

Ulanova's head was never found, nor her complete body, leading some to speculate that Samsonova not only killed her victims but cannibalized them. We will never know.

LIZZIE BORDEN – TAKES AN AXE

Did she or didn't she? According to her, she did not. But according to the schoolyard rhyme, she definitely did, even if the details were a little fanciful:

Lizzie Borden took an axe
And gave her mother forty whacks
And when she saw what she had done
She gave her father forty-one.

Lizzie Borden was the daughter of a well-to-do businessman from Fall River, Massachusetts, Andrew Jackson Borden. She was born in 1860 and her mother died when she was three. Her father was remarried three years later to a local woman named Abby Durfee Gray. Lizzie and her sister Emma were told to always call her Mrs Borden.

Andrew was known as a miser. Despite his wealth, the house had no plumbing, which was available at that time for the wealthy. He was also religious, and both his daughters were active in church matters; Lizzie taught at the Sunday school and was treasurer for the Christian Endeavor Society. She

DARK SECRETS

and Emma both lived at home and never married. Also in the house was a live-in maid named Bridget Sullivan, known to all as Maggie.

A family argument in July 1892 prompted both sisters to take extended vacations in New Bedford. This may have been about money. Andrew had started funnelling money and property to Abby's family. Four days before their deaths, the entire Borden household was violently ill but recovered.

On 4 August 1892, when Lizzie was 32, Maggie was working in the kitchen when Andrew left for his morning walk. Sometime between 9 a.m. and 10.30 a.m., Abby went upstairs to make the beds. As she did, she was attacked – struck on the side of the head with a hatchet. She fell face down on the floor, and her killer then struck her 17 more times on the back of her head.

Andrew returned from his walk, but his key jammed in the door so he knocked. Maggie went to open the door, and as she did, she claimed she'd heard Lizzie laughing, and that the laughter came from upstairs. Lizzie later denied this.

Maggie then headed up to the third floor to clean windows, leaving 60-year-old Andrew to take a nap on the sofa. At 11.10 a.m. Lizzie screamed and called from downstairs, "Maggie, come quick! Father's dead. Somebody came in and killed him." Maggie rushed downstairs to find Andrew's head completely split – later investigations would discover he had been hit between ten and 12 times with the hatchet. One of his eyes was completely in half.

When the police arrived, they cordoned off the house. In the basement, they found two hatchets, two axes and a hatchet-head with a broken handle. Lizzie was told she was a suspect. The next morning, a family friend saw Lizzie in the kitchen tearing up a dress. Lizzie told her she was going to burn it as it had paint on it.

On 11 August, Lizzie was arrested and charged with the murders of her father and stepmother. She was held in custody, and confined to a small cheerless cell for the next nine months. On 5 June 1893, she stood trial. It was noted that on 1 June, another axe murder had occurred in Fall River, and the details were very similar to what had happened at the Borden house.

The prosecution tried but failed to make a convincing case. All evidence presented was circumstantial and contained many contradictions, not just in Lizzie's testimony, but also in Maggie's. Lizzie's presence when the murders occurred could not be established with any certainty.

After an hour and a half of deliberation she was acquitted. She returned to the house and lived there for another 34 years – Maggie, unsurprisingly, no longer worked there – dying in 1927. At the time of her death, with her various inheritances, Borden was worth over $250,000 (equivalent to $5,884,000 in 2023).

By then the schoolyard rhyme inspired by the events in Fall River was well established. She must have heard it many times. Did she hate the sound of it? Or did she give a laugh – like the one Maggie heard coming from the top of the stairs in 1892?

AUDREY MARIE HILLEY – WIFE, MOTHER, MURDERER

Late in the summer of 1982, John Greenleaf Homan III received a phone call from a woman named Teri Martin. She was, she said, the sister of his wife, Robbi Hannon, who he had married a year earlier. She was sorry to tell him that Robbi had died while away tending to family business in Texas.

Homan was devastated. He and Teri stayed in touch and they started to feel a connection. A few months later, Teri came to visit Homan in New Hampshire. United in their grief, they became lovers – and Teri came to replace her sister Robbi in his affections.

Except Teri wasn't Robbi's sister. Teri *was* Robbi. She had changed her hair, lost weight and started dressing differently in order to return to the man she had left. That Teri and Robbi shared memories was no surprise. But what was surprising, as Homan was to find out later, was that these memories weren't real either. There was no real Teri Martin. There was no real Robbi Hannon. The woman pretending to be both sisters was named Audrey Marie Hilley, and for the last three years she had been on the run, believed to have murdered her husband Frank and attempted to murder her 15-year-old daughter, Carol.

Born Audrey "Marie" Frazier on 4 June 1933, she married Frank Hilley on 8 May 1951. They had two children, Mike and Carol, but despite Frank's good job and Marie doing secretarial work, they struggled financially as Marie spent their money as quickly as it came in. She was also, unbeknown to Frank, sleeping with a number of other men, including her bosses in order to get promotions, or simply for money.

In the early 1970s Frank began to suffer from stomach pains, as did his son Mike. The doctors put it down to stomach flu, but Frank's symptoms continued for longer than would be expected. Mike got better when he went to study to become a priest.

In May 1975, Frank's stomach problems got worse and worse. Earlier that year he had come home from work sick and found Marie in bed with her boss. His son, now an ordained minister, counselled forgiveness. It was a fatal piece of advice. On 24 May, Frank was rushed to hospital, where tests indicated a malfunction of the liver. He died the next morning. Doctors diagnosed infectious hepatitis, a diagnosis that the autopsy seemed to support – swelling of the kidneys and lungs, and inflammation of the stomach were consistent with hepatitis. Marie claimed a small life-insurance payout of $31,000.

Soon after, Marie took out life insurance on her 15-year-old daughter, Carol, this time for $50,000 – $25,000 for any death, and an extra $25,000 for accidental death. Almost immediately Carol started experiencing similar symptoms to her father, which made the doctors believe they were psychosomatic – she did not have hepatitis but was mirroring what Frank went through. It was later revealed that Marie also gave her a series of injections, forcing her to promise she would not tell anyone about them. Carol was taken to hospital for psychiatric assessment and the symptoms disappeared.

After Carol had spent a month in care, a number of test results came back to the hospital. The staff were shocked to find drastic vitamin deficiencies and a group of symptoms associated with malnutrition. She also had symptoms that were associated with heavy metal poisoning – nerve palsy, numb hands and feet, and a loss of reflexes. More tests revealed traces of arsenic in her fingernails and hair, over 100 times the normal level. On 9 October 1979, the hospital called 911, and a warrant was put out for the arrest of Marie Hilley.

But she was already in custody – for passing false cheques. Ironically, the cheques were to the insurance company invalidating the indemnity. A search revealed a vial in her handbag containing traces of arsenic. She was immediately charged with attempted murder. Astonishingly, one month later she was released on bail. Less astonishingly, she went on the run, pausing only to break into her aunt's house, steal money and clothes and take the car.

In her absence, Frank was exhumed, tested and found to have arsenic in his system. Her mother and mother-in-law had died with traces of arsenic, although it was inconclusive as the levels were not far above normal. And various family friends came forward to give evidence that they had become ill after spending time with Marie. She was charged in absentia with the death of Frank.

Three years passed. She became Robbi Hannon, married John Homan, faked her death, and then for reasons only known to herself, became Teri Martin and returned to her second husband. But as it became increasingly evident that the death notices placed in Robbi's name were fake, and as Homan's own business started to leak money without explanation, police grew suspicious of "Teri Martin" and figured out that she and Robbi were the same woman. They believed she was a petty thief they were searching for named Carol Manning. But when they took her in, they found that her true crimes were much more horrific. Extradited to Alabama, she received a life sentence for the murder of Frank and 20 years for the attempted murder of Carol.

But there was more. Four years into her sentence, having been a model prisoner, she was given a three-day pass to visit Homan, now remarried and living in Anniston, Alabama. The couple spent a day at a hotel. Homan woke to a note from her, asking for forgiveness. He called the police. Marie was gone again.

But this time not for long. She was found four days later. What had happened in that time remains a mystery, but she was discovered virtually naked on a nearby porch, delirious and covered in mud. Rushed to hospital, she lost consciousness and then suffered a massive heart attack, dying three and a half hours later. The diagnosis was hypothermia – she seemed to have been crawling around the woods for four days in often sub-zero temperatures.

What had happened to Marie Hilley, alias Robbi Hannon, alias Teri Martin? Was it something accidental? Had she just got lost? Or had the magnitude of her crimes finally caught up with her, and driven her out of her mind? That secret died with her.

KRISTEN GILBERT – THE ANGEL OF DEATH

The patient would not necessarily know what was happening. Once epinephrine, commonly known as adrenaline, is introduced via an intravenous bag in a sufficient amount, death through cardiac arrest occurs quickly, though those final few moments can be agonizing.

There had, of course, been suspicions – it did seem odd how many patients died during Kristen Gilbert's shifts at the Veterans Affairs Medical Center (VAMC) in Northampton, Massachusetts. Other nurses jokingly called her "The Angel of Death" – but even they would have been stunned that the chances of almost half of the hospital's 350 deaths being while she was on duty was 1 in 100 million. As investigators quickly showed, this was no coincidence.

Born Kristen Heather Strickland in Fall River, Massachusetts, on 13 November 1967, she was incredibly bright, graduating at 16. This was offset by an addiction to lying and her habit of indulging in a number of faked suicide attempts in order to manipulate friends and family. She also made violent threats against other teenagers.

In 1986, while at college, another fake suicide attempt saw her receive psychiatric treatment. But she continued her academic excellence and chose nursing, becoming a registered nurse in 1988. That same year she married Glenn Gilbert, and a year later she joined the staff of the VAMC. That's when the death rates started to go up.

By 1996, there were serious grounds for concern among the staff, and at least three nurses reported to management the frequency of cardiac incidents during Kristen's shifts. Not all of the patients died – some were in fact resuscitated by Kristen herself – but it still seemed very strange. Also strange was the decrease in the supply of available epinephrine. They kept running out, and its absence did not tally with medical records.

While an investigation was launched, Kristen checked herself into psychiatric hospitals seven times. She also issued an anonymous bomb threat against the VAMC, for what she would later say was revenge against the other nurses for participating in the investigation. It was this that she was initially arrested for.

Subsequently charged with murder, she pleaded innocent and thus gave no reason for the actions she claimed not to have committed. Other staff believed she was deliberately causing emergency situations in order to show off her ability to manage them, while there was also speculation that she was particularly keen to show off to James Perrault, a VA police officer with whom she was having an affair. Hospital rules required that hospital police be present at any medical emergency – perhaps she just wanted to spend more time with her lover and to impress him?

More and more evidence was produced, showing Kristen endangering the lives of patients – in 1995 she had left a patient who was having a cardiac arrest, and in 1996 she had removed a breathing tube from a patient, causing a medical emergency. On 14 March 2001, after six hours' deliberation, a jury convicted Kristen Gilbert on three counts of first-degree murder, one count of second-degree murder and two counts of attempted murder.

There is no death penalty in Massachusetts. However, a veterans' hospital is a federal jurisdiction, so the judge could have sentenced her to be executed. The defence argued strongly that all the evidence in the case was circumstantial – no one had ever seen Kristen carry out a murder. The judge decided on clemency of sorts, sentencing her to four consecutive life terms without the possibility of parole, plus 20 years. She also received 15 months for the bomb threat.

MARY BELL – THE CHILD

In May 1980, a convicted murderer was released from HM Prison Askham Grange in North Yorkshire, England. She had been locked up for 11 and a half years, having first been locked away in December 1968. Her name was Mary Bell, she was only 23 and had spent half her life behind bars.

Or at least, her name *was* Mary Bell. On her release, she was given a new name and granted lifelong anonymity. Her case had shocked an entire nation, and not everyone could be guaranteed to forgive. After all, it is not every day that a murderer turns out to be ten years old when she did it, let alone when she did it twice.

She was born on 26 May 1957. Her mother, Elizabeth "Betty" Bell, was 17 and a prostitute, specializing in sadomasochistic sex. Her father may or may not have been William Bell, a violent alcoholic and habitual criminal with an arrest record for crimes including armed robbery. When hospital staff had tried to present Betty with her newborn she yelled, "Take the thing away from me!"

Mary's childhood was abusive – she was either being neglected or beaten, and evidence points to the fact that her mother may have actually been trying to kill her. She was once dropped from a first-floor window, another time given an overdose of sleeping pills. Mary's mother even sold her once – Mary's older sister had to go and get her back.

Unable to get rid of the child, Betty Bell included her in her activities with clients, encouraging several of her clients to sexually abuse Mary in sadomasochistic sessions by the mid-1960s, when she was under ten.

Unsurprisingly, Mary was subject to violent mood swings at school and, increasingly, violent acts. On 11 May 1968, she pushed a three-year-old off a roof. Her friend Norma Bell (no relation) later told police that Mary had also tried "throttling" the girl, having asked her, "What happens if you choke someone; do they die?" Then, said Norma, "Mary put both hands round the girl's throat and squeezed. The girl started to go purple."

Then on 25 May, the day before her eleventh birthday, Mary was playing with four-year-old Martin Brown in a derelict house in Newcastle. This time the throttling didn't stop. Brown was found lying on his back with his arms stretched above his head, with blood and foam around his mouth. No sign of strangulation could be found; Mary's hands were too small for anything to show. The cause of death was a mystery, and the whole community was mystified.

The next day, Mary's birthday, she and her friend Norma vandalized a nursery school near home. A series of notes was left behind, including one which read, "WE did murder martain [sic] brown f***of [sic] you bastard". It was dismissed as a prank.

Then on 31 July, three-year-old Brian Howe was seen playing outside with Mary and Norma. When he failed to come home in the evening, a search party was organized. At 11.10 p.m., Brian's body was discovered, wedged between two large concrete blocks. He had bruises and cuts, and a pair of scissors with a bent blade was found nearby.

The autopsy discovered that he had been dead for seven and a half hours and had been killed by being strangled with his nose held closed. His genitals had been mutilated, his legs cut and a crude "M" carved into his chest. The police initially thought the killer was an adult, but the coroner pointed to the lack of force used. He told shocked police that the killer seemed to be another child.

More than 1,200 children from all around the local area were questioned, Mary and Norma included – a hugely traumatic event for the community. Both Mary and Norma admitted playing with him in the morning but not in the afternoon. But Mary made a crucial error. She told them she had seen another boy hitting Brian Howe. The boy had scissors she told them. She said she saw him trying to cut a cat's tail off, but one leg of the scissors was broken or bent. The fact that the scissors found at the murder scene were bent was only known to the police. Also, the boy she mentioned was known to have been away at the time of the killing. Police knew Mary was the killer.

It was Norma who came forward – her parents told the police she had something to tell them. Mary had told her about the murder and even told her where she had hidden a razor blade she used on Howe's stomach. The razor blade was where she said it would be.

The funeral of Brian Howe took place on 7 August. Mary Bell was under constant surveillance as evidence was gathered. As Howe's coffin passed Mary's house, one of the police officers assigned to the case saw her outside. "She stood there, laughing. Laughing and rubbing her hands. I thought, 'My

God, I've got to bring her in. She'll do another one.'" At 8 p.m. that evening, Mary and Norma were both arrested.

Mary immediately blamed Norma for the murders, but it was obvious to all which of the girls was telling the truth and which was lying. Mary was clearly the dominant partner in the relationship, and the cunning she had shown in luring her victims into her trap failed in adult company. She was denied the right to anonymity, with the newspapers soon calling Mary the "Most Evil Child in Britain".

The trial lasted nine days. Norma was acquitted, but Mary was found guilty of manslaughter on the grounds of diminished responsibility – even the most evil child in Britain could not be expected to know the full consequences of her actions. It made little difference to the sentence, though. The judge described Mary as a "dangerous" individual, adding that she posed a "very grave risk to other children", and sentenced her to be detained indefinitely at Her Majesty's pleasure, first in a young offenders' institute – she was the only girl among 24 inmates and later claimed to be sexually abused by staff and other prisoners – and then in HM Prison Askham Grange.

So, when she emerged into the daylight in May 1980, Mary had only known prison for half her life. In 1984, she had a daughter, and the pair were protected from the glare of the media.

For a while at least. In 1998, a newspaper tracked them down to a house in Sussex, and the pair were forced to flee to a safe house with bedsheets over their heads, before having their identities changed again and being sent to a new location. It was the first time Mary's daughter would know her mother's true identity.

In 2003, they won the legal right to permanent anonymity, which includes Mary's granddaughter. Divulging any information that might lead to their identification is now illegal.

Interviewed many years later, the mother of Martin Brown told a reporter about a recurring dream of her boy in a blue anorak like the one Martin was wearing the day he died, "and I am trying and trying to turn him round so I can see his face, but I can't. I want him back so badly and I can't get to him."

IRINA GAIDAMACHUK – SATAN IN A SKIRT

There are many ways to kill – an injection, strangulation, a gunshot. Irina Gaidamachuk was no subtle murderess – her weapons of choice were brutally simple. She favoured smashing in the heads of her 17 victims with a hammer or an axe.

She gave various reasons for her crimes, but all of them circled back to one motive: to get money to buy alcohol, which her husband Yuri would not let her have. Her addiction to vodka was overpowering and had been with her all her life. She was born in the Soviet Union town of Nyagan, Khanty–Mansi Autonomous Okrug, on 22 May 1972. Her life was chaotic from the start. Her parents were both alcoholics and lost custody of Gaidamachuk at a young age.

She married Yuri in her early 20s and they had two children, but even this could not stop her craving the demon drink.

Gaidamachuk's murder spree began in 2002, and she attacked elderly women, using the bluntest of instruments to open their skulls. She then took what money she could, sometimes burning down their house before she left, making it look like an accident. The money was then spent on vodka.

She never went far in order to commit her crimes – most occurred in her home town of Krasnoufimsk or those that surrounded it. Despite this, police, who had linked the crimes to one perpetrator, struggled to find who the killer was – they assumed it was a male. It wasn't until 2010, when one woman managed to escape and describe her attacker, that they were able to shift their attention. They immediately arrested a female suspect, 29-year-old Marina Valeyeva, who confessed to the murders under interrogation, the final of nearly 3,000 wrong arrests generated by the case.

But soon after, when Gaidamachuk killed Alexandra Povaritsyna after posing as a painter offering to do house decoration, a positive identification was given by a neighbour. Gaidamachuk was arrested and confessed immediately, giving the police a full description of her crimes. Handwriting at the scene of a number of the murders corroborated her story. Valeyeva was set free, and Gaidamachuk, dubbed "Satan in a Skirt" by the media, was charged with 17 counts of murder and one of attempted murder.

Despite the horror of her crimes, few had achieved her stated aim of making her lots of money. Court estimates showed a tiny amount, and all of it had been spent on vodka. It made each life only worth a few bottles.

She was sentenced to the maximum term for a woman in Russia – a mere 20 years, only just over one year per victim. A short sentence... but a long, long time without a drink.

STACEY CASTOR – THE BLACK WIDOW

"He's not dead, he's not dead!" In August 2005, when Sergeant Robert Willoughby kicked in the door of the bedroom of David Castor, he was accompanied by Stacey Castor screaming that her husband must be alive. But it did not take much of an inspection to see that he was dead, and that on the bedside table was a half-full glass of bright green liquid, another glass that had some remnants of some juice, and an apricot brandy bottle. Underneath the bed was a bottle of antifreeze.

Willoughby was there because David's wife had called the police to say she was worried about him, as she said he had locked himself in the bedroom all day, suffering from a bout of depression. When he failed to respond to Willoughby calling through the door, the police officer had kicked it down and found the body. The coroner ruled that David had committed suicide.

It was the second time Stacey Castor had been widowed in her 38 years. Born Stacey Daniels in New York in 1967, she had met and married her first husband, Michael Wallace, in 1985 when she was 17. They had two daughters, Ashley in 1988 and Bree in 1991. The couple gradually grew apart, both having extramarital affairs as the relationship soured. Interviewed in 2009, Stacey said that Wallace had become addicted to alcohol and drugs.

In late 1999, Wallace's health deteriorated rapidly. He was unsteady on his feet, his speech was slurred and medical authorities diagnosed an inner-ear infection. No treatment worked. In early 2000, he was found unresponsive on their sofa by 12-year-old Ashley. Rushed to hospital, he was pronounced dead soon after. Inexplicably, no autopsy was ordered, despite the strangeness of an – until then – mostly healthy 38-year-old dying so suddenly. The doctors simply ascribed it to a heart attack. Stacey received $55,000 in life insurance.

In 2003, she married David, and she and her two daughters joined him and his own son, David Jnr. The daughters were, according to Stacey, resistant to the marriage. She said they didn't want their father replaced. Moreover, David was difficult with the kids, expecting them to always do what he wanted, which her daughters refused to do.

Then in 2005, Willoughby received the call. He proceeded to the Castor house for a "wellness check" of David, and was confronted by the dead body and a screaming Stacey. Once the Castors – one dead and one alive – were removed from the scene, authorities carried out a more extensive search of the property. As well as the antifreeze under the bed, they found a turkey baster lying in the garbage can in the kitchen.

Willoughby said he noticed it had droplets inside it. "So I pick it up and I pull the rubber ball off it and I smell it and I can smell alcohol in it… I know alcohol is involved. I know that antifreeze is involved."

Fingerprints were taken of the bottles, glasses and the baster. The prints of Stacey Castor were all over them. "The fingerprints [were] in such a way that it was as if someone held the glass from the bottom," said Detective Dominick Spinelli, who worked on the case. This implied it had been fed to David. Antifreeze was found on the turkey baster, as was David's DNA.

And then there was the will. David had left everything to his wife and her two daughters – but nothing to his beloved son. Police suspicions grew.

Meanwhile, David had been buried, on Stacey's bizarre instructions, right next to her first husband, Michael Wallace. The pair had no connection apart from their wife.

In 2007, detectives were allowed to exhume Wallace and perform an autopsy, and what they found was shocking. His organs were covered in crystals – a known reaction caused by antifreeze. It seems that Stacey had used the same method to kill both her husbands.

And then, if possible, she did something worse. On finding out that the police had discovered traces of antifreeze in Wallace, she decided to frame her daughter, Ashley, then 19, for the murders. The police had contacted Ashley on her first day of college to inform her that her father had been poisoned. She called Stacey, who invited her home to comfort her. She offered Ashley a "nasty-tasting" alcoholic drink, which Ashley refused and then sipped.

The next day, with what she thought was a hangover, Ashley returned to college, then returned home to her mother, and they drank together again. Seventeen hours later her sister Bree found Ashley passed out. She forced her mother to call the paramedics, and when they arrived, Stacey handed them a suicide note from Ashley, confessing to killing her father and stepfather.

Ashley had been 15 minutes from death, her body filled with a cocktail of drugs. She had no knowledge of trying to kill herself, or of writing any note. She certainly had not killed her father or stepfather.

By then they had already arrested Stacey Castor, now dubbed "The Black Widow" in the press, and charged her with two counts of murder, one of attempted murder, and one of forging a will. She was tried in 2009, showing no emotion, even when Ashley appeared as a witness. The jury took only four days to find her guilty on all counts. She was sentenced to 51 years in prison. She died there in 2016.

"She was my best friend," said Ashley. "And then she took that all away… I would have done anything for her, but she decided she wanted to kill me instead."

STELLA NICKELL – THE TAMPERER

Early on 11 June 1986, 40-year-old bank manager Sue Snow took two Excedrin painkiller capsules for an early-morning headache. Her husband, Paul Webking, who suffered from arthritis, also took two tablets, and then headed off to work. At 6.30 a.m., the couple's daughter, Hayley, found her mother collapsed on the bathroom floor. Paramedics were called and Snow was rushed to hospital. She died without regaining consciousness.

An autopsy revealed the presence of cyanide in her body, which were traced back to the Excedrin tablets she had taken that morning. Of the 60 tablets still in the bottle, three contained traces of cyanide. The manufacturers of Excedrin immediately recalled the product, and when another tainted bottle was found in a nearby Seattle grocery store, a group of drug companies came together to offer a $300,000 reward for the capture of the person responsible.

On 19 June, Stella Nickell from Washington contacted police. Her husband Bruce had also died suddenly after taking Excedrin, and she turned two bottles of the drug over to investigators. An autopsy by the FDA revealed that he too had died of cyanide poisoning. Both bottles were also found to contain the poison.

A huge investigation of the Excedrin factory was carried out, and no traces of cyanide were found there. At the same time, another contaminated bottle was found, but this was in a separate drug, Anacin-3. The manufacturer of Excedrin was cleared of suspicion – this was clearly a case of product tampering on the shelves. The sale of all non-prescription medication was banned for 90 days. Occurring just a few years after the unsolved Chicago Tylenol-tampering incident, in which at least seven died, the new deaths caused shock across the US.

The FBI crime lab carried out more extensive tests on the cyanide and found that it was from an algaecide called Algae Destroyer used in home fish tanks. It was obvious that someone had tampered with the bottles and placed them back on the shelf. The spouses of Bruce Nickell and Sue Snow were asked to take polygraph tests. Paul Webking agreed immediately. But Stella Nickell refused.

Bruce Nickell was Stella's second husband. She was born in Oregon in 1943, and her childhood had been an unhappy one, being brought up in a poor family. She had her first child, Cynthia, at 16, and another soon after by her first husband. Now living in Southern California, she had previous convictions for beating her daughter with a curtain rod and or forgery. The latter landed her in prison for six months in 1971 and ended her marriage.

She met Bruce in 1974, and they married in 1976. He was a heavy-equipment operator who drank a lot, but during their marriage he entered rehab and became sober. Stella would later say that she now found him boring. She continued drinking heavily and took up new pastimes and hobbies – including keeping fish.

Her refusal to take the polygraph stirred the interest of the police. They also discovered that she had recently taken out $76,000 in life insurance on her husband. Even more incriminating was the fact it became clear that the two contaminated bottles of Excedrin that she handed in had been purchased at different times and different stores – the chances of her randomly buying two of the very few contaminated bottles were miniscule. The police were convinced that Stella was the killer but needed more than circumstantial evidence.

In November 1986, she finally assented to a polygraph. And failed it. At the same time, it was discovered that she had borrowed a number of library books about poisons, including Human Poisoning from Native and Cultivated Plants and Deadly Harvest, which she never returned. A fingerprint test showed the most prints on pages about cyanide.

It was then that her now grown-up daughter Cynthia presented herself to the authorities. She had been wrestling with her conscience. Her mother had spoken to her numerous times about killing Bruce because she was bored with him, and had even tried once before, by placing foxglove in his medication, but it had only made him drowsy. She had also told Cynthia what she planned to do with the inheritance and insurance money when he died.

On 9 December 1987, Stella Nickell was charged with the murder of Bruce Nickell and Sue Snow, as well as with the new crime of product tampering, instituted after the Chicago Tylenol incidents. The separate bottles had of course been a decoy – by planting them, Stella hoped to fool law enforcement into thinking that it was a random incident that led to the death of her husband.

Found guilty on all charges, Stella Nickell was sentenced to two terms of 90 years for the deaths of her husband and Sue Snow, and to three ten-year sentences for the known cases of tampering. No one knows how many other bottles she tampered with, or if anyone else suffered the consequences. What we do know is that she was prepared for others to die in order to succeed in her evil deed.

LOUISE VERMILYA – THE UNDERTAKER

She just seemed to like seeing dead people. When *The New York Times* interviewed local Barrington, Illinois undertaker E. N. Blocks in 1911, shortly after Louise Vermilya had been arrested, he told them that she was constantly visiting his mortuary, even asking if she could work for him. She was a constant presence at his mortuary. "At every death she would seem to hear of it just as soon as I, and she would reach the house only a little behind me," said Blocks.

Born in 1868, Vermilya managed to get through the first 25 years of her life without killing anyone, although she would more than make up for it over the next 20. At 16 she married 24-year-old Fred Brinkamp, and her husband became her first victim when she poisoned him on their farm in 1893. The coroner delivered a finding of heart attack, and no autopsy was performed. Vermilya collected $5,000 in life insurance, but unlike several other women who murdered their husbands, it quickly became clear that this was not her main motivation.

The couple had six children, and within a year eight-year-old Cora was also dead, followed by her little sister, four-and-a-half-year-old Florence. Given the high rates of infant mortality at the time, little was thought of it, although some said the family was cursed. But if it was a curse, it seemed to have been lifted – for the next 13 years no one died.

That changed when the widow Vermilya moved to Chicago in 1906, taking her remaining four children with her. There she met up with a relative of Fred's, 26-year-old Lillian Brinkamp. Vermilya killed her too, perhaps just for old times' sake.

She then married a 59-year-old man named Charles Vermilya, whose name she took, and who had an adult stepson. Three years later both were dead. Still keeping it in the family, next to go was her 23-year-old son from her first marriage, Frank Brinkamp. Having just been awarded $1,200 in divorce proceedings, he fell ill. It is said that on his deathbed he told his new fiancée that he was "going the same way my father did," raising the possibility that the family suspected Vermilya was involved in the deaths.

Perhaps if Vermilya had stuck to family, she may have gotten away with her work – the idea of the family curse provided some cover. But by now she had a taste for killing. On 15 January 1910, Jason Rupert, a railroad fireman, fell ill after having dinner with Vermilya. Two days later he was dead. She had started taking in boarders, and it is known that some of them never left, but record-keeping wasn't her strength, so the numbers are unknown.

In February 1911, Vermilya married one of her boarders, Richard Smith, a train conductor, and in March 1911 she killed him. What she didn't know was that Smith was a bigamist, and his other wife raised her suspicions. She thought her estranged husband had been murdered for his money, although Vermilya never really seemed to care about that. She also put forward the idea that Vermilya had killed him because the local undertaker, a C. C. Boysen, was jealous of another man winning her affections! If she wished to stop Boysen being jealous, could there be any better way than disposing of the rival, and giving him some business?

It was now only a matter of time before she was caught. In October 1911, she invited a local father and son, the Bissonettes, over for dinner. During the meal the son, Arthur, began to experience abdominal pains, then dropped dead. When the coroner investigated the case, Arthur's father noted that he had seen Vermilya adding what looked like white pepper to their meals, but not hers.

Vermilya was placed under house arrest on 28 October. Strangely, she was allowed to continue preparing her own meals. Realizing she faced the death penalty, she began adding "white pepper" to the dishes, and by 9 December she was paralyzed and suffering from heart problems. Although she made a partial recovery, once indicted she attended court in a wheelchair.

She was charged with only two deaths, that of Arthur Bissonette and her husband of just a month, Rupert Smith. Both had high doses of arsenic in their corpses. However, the prosecutors decided not to pursue the Bissonette case when it was discovered that he had been taking medication which also contained traces of arsenic. While it was unlikely that this could have caused his death, it made the case more complicated, and it was felt it would be easier to convict her of the murder of Smith, which would lead to the death penalty anyway.

The trial began on 21 March 1912 and did not go smoothly. Vermilya again attempted suicide, delaying the case. Jury selection was difficult as many men refused to be part of a jury that might sentence a woman to death. Also, the trial had been such big news that very few men could be found who did not already have an opinion, jeopardizing the chance of a fair hearing. Come June 1913, Vermilya was still in custody – and her failing health was becoming an issue. It was decided she should be released on bail.

Two years later, it was decided by Assistant State Attorney Sullivan and State Attorney Hoyne that the chances of securing a conviction were almost nil. In Sullivan's words, "We could only see that another trial would entail a heavy cost without any assurance of being able to show any strong evidence." All charges were dropped, and Louise Vermilya was never heard of again.

TILLIE KLIMEK – THE FORTUNE TELLER

For thousands of years, humans have wondered about psychic abilities – how is it that some people are able to communicate by thought, move objects using only brain power, talk to ghosts and spectres, and predict the future? Are there, as Hamlet says, more things in heaven and earth than are dreamed of in our philosophies? Or might there be something else going on?

The early twentieth century was a time of huge psychic activity and unrest – seances, table-turning and other occult activities were in vogue across all classes, and all around the world. The theosophy of Madame Blavatsky, the popularity of tarot cards and the paranormal investigations of writers like Arthur Conan Doyle, the creator of Sherlock Holmes, captured a moment where the supernatural exploded into the natural world.

Enter Tillie Klimek. Born Otylia Gburek in 1876 in Poland, her parents emigrated to the US when she was four years old and settled in the "Little Poland" district of Chicago. In 1895, the 19 year old married Jozef "Joe" Mitkiewicz, and they appeared to be a happy couple.

Tillie was a strong personality in the local community, renowned for her cooking and for certain psychic abilities, particularly in the realm of augury – predicting the future. There is a strong tradition in Polish folk customs of clairvoyance and Tillie seemed to have acquired the ability.

Sometime in 1914, though, her clairvoyance took a disturbing turn. She told friends and neighbours that she was having visions of Joe dying, and they were getting stronger. A few weeks later he died of heart trouble. Tillie's vision had come true.

Soon after, she remarried – another Joe – Joseph Ruskowski. Again, she had visions of his death, again they came true, as did visions she had of another man who was known to have jilted her.

By now, such was Tillie's confidence in her abilities that when she started having visions of the death of her third husband, Frank Kupczyk, she was quite open with him about it, often saying to him, "You'll be dying soon," and "Not long now, Frank." She even started tailoring her own mourning clothes and hat as they sat down of an evening, and bought a coffin that she had found for sale. Sure enough, in 1921, despite being in robust health, Frank passed away, just as Tillie had said he would.

She married a fourth husband, and third Joe – Joseph Klimek – later that year. Again, the visions started, and her third Joe fell ill. But this time doctors intervened, suspecting arsenic poisoning. Tests confirmed this was the case, and Tillie Klimek was arrested.

Also arrested was her cousin Nellie. Nellie had given Tillie rat poison called "Rough on Rats" when Tillie had told her she was bored with Frank. Exhumation of Frank's body revealed he too had died of arsenic poisoning – in fact, all of Tillie's dead husbands and boyfriends had. She was not so much predicting their deaths as scheduling them.

It soon became clear that it was not just those whose deaths Tillie had predicted who had bitten the dust. Lots of her neighbours and relatives had also fallen ill and died – as well as one dog that had annoyed her. In all, 20 people were found to have been poisoned by Tillie, and 14 had died.

It also became apparent that Tillie had not necessarily acted alone. A number of her neighbours were also arrested. The papers spoke of a clique of wives in Little Poland who were bumping off their husbands. Tillie was, however, the "high priestess".

Nellie spent a year in prison before she was acquitted, while Tillie received a life sentence.

AMELIA DYER – THE OGRESS OF READING

In 1869, when Amelia Dyer – a trained nurse, newly widowed – needed some cash, she turned to a new and lucrative trade that had just begun in Victorian England: adopting babies for money, baby farming. The trade was popular at a time when being an unwed mother was social death. Dyer took on several children, and business was good. Too good – after all, there are only so many children you can fit into a small house, and only so many mouths you can feed.

Born in 1837, near Bristol in England, she was the youngest of five children and, as everyone said, the smartest. She loved reading, poetry especially. When her mother caught typhus, Dyer nursed her through her physical and mental suffering. It took a great toll on her, and she became estranged from her family, who had not given her any help.

At 24 she married 59-year-old George Thomas. Secure in her new life, she trained as a nurse and a midwife. But when he died in 1869, she lost both a husband and an income. She needed to find a way to survive.

She began baby farming. She would take in unwanted babies, from any class, for good payment. But like many in the trade,

Dyer struggled to make the money pay for the upkeep of the child. And like many in the trade she recognized a dead child was less costly than a living one. Most chose neglect to move the process along; Dyer was in more of a hurry. She strangled hers and then threw them in London's River Thames.

She had remarried in 1872, to a William Dyer. It was about this time she started killing children – we cannot know if William was aware. The police kept a close eye, and when they became too intrusive, she would fake mental illness and hide in an asylum. Then when the coast was clear, she would emerge and go back to work. She was also, as police records show, drinking heavily and taking opium.

In 1879 she was sentenced to six months' hard labour after being found guilty on a charge of neglect. A doctor had become suspicious of her activities and reported the matter to the authorities. Also, a dead child, Helena Fry, was found in the Thames wrapped in a parcel, with Dyer's address on it. However, the evidence was circumstantial, and Dyer was released.

She went back to work, but her intake of alcohol and drugs increased, and her need for money did too.

Time was running out. In January 1896, she had taken into her care the baby of 25-year-old barmaid Evelina Marmon, who hoped Dyer would look after her child until she could afford to buy her back. The pair exchanged numerous letters as the mother saved up to re-buy her baby. What Marmon didn't know was that Dyer had killed the child within two days of taking her, wrapping dressmaking tape around her neck.

The day after killing baby Marmon, she strangled another child, 13-month-old Harry Simmons. The two babies were placed in a carpet bag weighed down with rocks and thrown into the Thames. The bag was found shortly after, and the police were able to identify it belonged to Dyer, whose alias "Mrs Thomas" had been cracked.

On 3 April they raided Dyer's house, which stank of human decomposition. No remains were found, but the dressmaking tape Dyer usually used to kill the babies was there. The tape, as Dyer later admitted, was how it was possible to tell it was one she had killed. Six more babies were found dead in the Thames a day later, all with the same tape around their necks. A young woman was sent to Dyer as a decoy, to ask for her help in getting rid of a child. When Dyer went for the second meeting she was greeted by detectives and arrested.

Her trial began in early May 1896. Her own daughter testified against her. Dyer confessed but pleaded insanity – she presented the cases of her incarceration in asylums as evidence. The judge and jury were not convinced. Each incarceration matched moments when she was under heavy suspicion with the police and they were seen as a ploy to avoid arrest.

It took the jury less than five minutes to find her guilty and sentence her to death. In prison she filled five exercise books with what she called her last true and only confession. When a priest visited her cell on the morning of the execution and asked if she had anything to say, she simply handed him the books. She was hanged on 10 June 1896.

Although she was only charged with six deaths, most believed that more than 400 children had been killed by her hand. The case sent horror through the UK, still reeling from the Jack the Ripper killings, and she became the subject of a popular ballad:

DARK SECRETS

The old baby farmer, the wretched Miss Dyer
At the Old Bailey her wages is paid.
In times long ago, we'd a made a big fy-er
And roasted so nicely that wicked old jade.

Her ghost was said to haunt Newgate Prison where she died and was buried, in an unmarked grave, beneath its flagstones. Some 1,169 people were executed at Newgate, but it was Amelia Dyer, the Ogress of Reading, who was unable to find her rest.

LEONARDA CIANCIULLI – THE SOAP-MAKER OF CORREGGIO

It was a fortune teller who first got into Leonarda Cianciulli's head and set her on her path. Cianciulli had been born in 1894 and dreamed of a big family. The fortune teller told her that while she would have many children, all would die young.

The fortune teller did say one other thing that puzzled her for a long time: "In your right hand I see prison, in your left a criminal asylum." It would turn out to be as prophetic as her first declaration.

Sure enough, Cianciulli became pregnant 17 times but had three miscarriages. Ten more died in their youth. Cianciulli ascribed this to a curse her mother had put on her for marrying the wrong man, and it meant that she was fiercely protective of her four remaining children. She would do anything to protect them.

When her eldest son Giuseppe was drafted by the Italian army at the start of World War Two in 1939, she was terrified for him. She believed that the only way to protect him was through magic, and there was only one magic that would do. Human sacrifice. Her victims were quickly chosen, three neighbours who were all desperate to leave the provincial

DARK SECRETS

boredom of Correggio. Cianciulli told them she would find them husbands far from Correggio.

The first was Faustina Setti. Cianciulli told her that a husband was waiting for her in the province of Pola. She should tell no one about this, but she should, before leaving, write a series of postcards to her friends telling them she was in Pola, as a sign of her commitment to the move. She was to bring them and show them to Cianciulli before she left.

When Setti came over with the postcards, Cianciulli dragged her inside and drove an axe into her over and over. Then she cut the body into nine pieces, gathering her blood in a basin. She threw the remains in a pot and added caustic soda until the pieces dissolved and she was able to pour the mixture into a septic tank. But she kept the blood. This was what she needed to protect her son.

She said later that she had waited until it had coagulated and dried it in the oven. Then she ground it and mixed it with flour, sugar, chocolate, milk and eggs, as well as a bit of margarine, kneading all the ingredients together, making lots of crunchy tea cakes. These she served to any visitors, although she and Giuseppe also ate them. She also claimed Setti's life savings. And sent the postcards to Setti's friends.

Next up was Francesca Soavi. Her method was the same. Cianciulli assured her she had found her a husband, and a job at a school in the city of Piacenza. Again, she was made to write postcards. And again, she was killed with an axe, her body dissected, and her blood made into tea cakes. Cianciulli again earned a tidy sum.

Her third and final victim was Virginia Cacioppo, a retired opera singer who had fallen on hard times, despite having sung at La Scala. Cianciulli promised her a job as a secretary to an opera impresario in Florence. On 30 September 1940, Cacioppo, again sworn to secrecy, came to visit. She was also killed by an axe and chopped up into pieces, ready for the pot.

The opera singer may have been bigger than the others, as there were some of her remains left over. Adding a little cologne, Cianciulli said she was able to make some creamy soap. These she gave as gifts to friends and family.

Even better, when she used the blood of Cacioppo for tea cakes, they were better than her other batches. She said that the woman was really sweet.

It was the opera singer's sister-in-law who grew suspicious and alerted police. It became evident that she had last been seen entering Cianciulli's flat. The flat was searched and police found traces of human remains. At first Cianciulli denied everything, but when the police started to include Giuseppe in their investigations, she confessed, giving detailed descriptions of the slaughter.

She was found guilty on all three counts and sentenced to 30 years in prison and three years in a criminal asylum, just as the fortune teller had predicted. She died in 1970 while in the asylum, at the age of 76.

As for Guiseppe, whom she believed could only be kept safe by human sacrifice, he did indeed survive the war and lived to a ripe old age – the father of five children.

GWENDOLYN GRAHAM AND CATHERINE WOOD – LETHAL LOVERS

Catherine Wood was 24 and just coming out of a severe depression that had seen her weight reach 450 pounds (200 kilograms) after her seven-year marriage broke up. She had been hired a year earlier by the Alpine Manor nursing home and had risen to become a supervisor. She was Gwendolyn Graham's boss when they fell for each other.

Graham, aged 23, was born in California but brought up in Texas and was known for being quiet and always having a sad face.

Theirs was an intense affair. Wood had slimmed down and the pair partied at bars together. They also started engaging in risky sexual acts, such as asphyxiating each other to achieve better orgasms. Graham got a kick out of tying Wood down and covering her face with a pillow until she trembled and almost blacked out. She would hold the pillow there for longer and longer.

But it wasn't enough. They always had to stop before things became properly interesting. They needed someone who they could actually kill.

In the nursing home there were plenty of potential victims, many of whom had been abandoned by friends and family and were close to death anyway. Wood later said that it was Graham who first came up with the idea, and she initially thought it was just dirty talk during sex. But Graham was serious. They could make a game of it. They could kill women in order, so their initials spelled MURDER. Wood agreed.

Unfortunately for them, the first victims of their assaults proved too resilient, managing to fight them off. The game was abandoned for the day, but even the thrill of attempted murder had provided a sexual high. They chose as their next attempt a woman with Alzheimer's, who could not fight back. Wood said she acted as a lookout, one eye on the nurse's station and the other watching the killing. Graham pressed a washcloth on the woman's nose and mouth, holding it there until she gave the same tremble Wood did during asphyxiation sex. Wood watched, expecting Graham to stop. Graham did not. She kept going until the woman stopped trembling.

It was to be the first of at least five murders, although it may have been as many as 12. According to Wood, the method was always the same – she acted as lookout while Graham killed the woman. They got such a rush from the killings that they usually went straight to any empty room and had sex while reliving what they had done and listening for when the body was discovered. Graham always took a souvenir of the murder, which she kept on a shelf, which became part of their sex play.

The murders did not appear suspicious, and both Graham and Wood were well-respected by workmates. But like so many murderers, hubris was their enemy. Graham began increasing the risk, bragging to other staff about what they were doing and even showing off the souvenirs. Other staff just thought it was gallows humour, some kind of sick joke.

According to Wood, it was in April 1987 that Graham said it was time for Wood to prove her love and carry out one of the murders. Wood said she couldn't. Graham broke off the relationship immediately – in fact she had already fallen for someone else. She left the nursing home to go with her new lover, Heather Barager, back to her home state of Texas.

Wood's anger and guilt became too much for her. She told her ex-husband what she and Graham had done, and he called the police straight away.

At first the police didn't believe Wood – there had been 40 deaths at the home that year, none of them regarded as suspicious at the time. Closer investigation revealed that eight were in fact highly suspicious, five of which the pair ended up being charged with. Graham and Wood were both arrested in December 1988, with Wood turning state witness to reduce her sentence. She received 20 to 40 years, depending on behaviour, and was released in 2020. Graham received five life sentences. Justice had been served, people felt.

But there was a twist. In 1992, the renowned writer Lowell Cauffiel released a book about the case, *Forever and Five Days*. He spoke to friends, co-workers, family members and others who knew Graham and Wood. Many of them told a completely different story. Wood, they said, was a pathological liar who had spent her life ruining the lives of others. The book claimed that Wood had planned the first murder to stop Graham leaving her after seeing Graham with another woman. She then continued to kill, persuading Graham to assist her.

But then Graham left her anyway. Wood, according to the book, exacted her revenge by confessing and then turning witness. Psychological testing of Graham revealed she suffered from borderline personality disorder and was easily manipulated. She was also regarded – based on her inability to defend herself at the trial – as unlikely to have been able to plan a series of murders. Wood had been the murderer, the book says, and she framed Graham as revenge for leaving her.

The book also raised one other possibility, based on conversations that Wood had engaged in with other inmates after incarceration. She had told them something which, if true, is as shocking as anything else in this story. There were, Wood said, no murders at all. She had made the whole thing up to destroy Graham's life after she had gone off with another woman.

Would someone really condemn themselves to years in prison to get back at a former lover?

If Gwendolyn Graham is right about Wood, then maybe.

REVENGE AND RETRIBUTION

It is said that "revenge is a dish best served cold". But as the women in this chapter show, it can still be pretty good served lukewarm or piping hot. Why wait, when you can serve it up now?

For some women, such as Olga Hepnarová, revenge and retribution were not against any one person – it was society itself that had to suffer for what she had been through. It was the same with Brenda Ann Spencer on that fateful Monday in January 1979, a day of the week that she famously said she didn't like. The victims were unknown to her. They weren't the ones she wanted revenge against, but they were part of a world she did want to suffer her wrath.

Sylvia Seegrist might have sympathized with Hepnarová and Spencer if they ever had a chance to get to know each other. She opened fire in a shopping mall, but her anger was directed at the same thing – the world. The world was shocked, and Seegrist was locked away for life.

Sometimes a murder is about honour, as in the case of Shi Jianqiao, who tracked down her father's killer and put him to death; sometimes it's about an ideal, like when Charlotte Corday killed Jean-Paul Marat as revenge for the extremes that the French Revolution had begun to engage in. Corday believed her actions would stop a civil war – none happened so perhaps she was right.

But for the most part, revenge works best in the home, or failing that, in the home of the woman the victim left the killer for. Did Betty Broderick know she was going to kill her ex-husband and his new, younger wife when she broke into their house carrying a gun? She says no, but the jury said yes. If "hell hath no fury like a woman scorned", then hell appears a very peaceful place compared to what happened in the San Diego bedroom of Dan Broderick.

And if a killer doesn't have a gun, a car will do. In fairness, Clara Suarez Harris had begun by trying to fight her husband and his lover as they emerged into the foyer of the hotel the private investigator had seen them at, but when she was ejected, running them over in her Mercedes seemed a logical option. The end of the affair, very abruptly.

The desire for revenge can be deep-seated, or it can be a feeling that passes quickly. But murder is forever. Did the women in this chapter ever come to regret their crimes? Was what happened to them worse than the feeling of betrayal they felt? One thinks not, and yet they won't be the last to go down this terrible path.

BETTY BRODERICK – A WOMAN SCORNED

Shortly before dawn on 5 November 1989, Betty Broderick drove to the Georgian-style mansion of her ex-husband Dan in downtown San Diego. She was two days short of her 42nd birthday. She had her daughter Kim's keys to the house with her. She also had a .38, five-shot revolver.

Climbing the stairs, she entered the bedroom where Dan was sleeping with his new wife, Linda. She fired five shots, as she recalled, with no hesitation at all. One hit a bedside table. One hit a wall. But the other three hit the sleeping couple. One went through Linda's neck and into her brain, while another went into her chest. The final bullet went into Dan's back, perforating his lung.

He didn't die immediately. "Okay, okay, you got me," he said to Betty and then rolled off the bed onto the floor and started crawling towards a telephone. Betty grabbed the phone and yanked it out of the wall. She took one last look at her dying ex-husband and left.

Betty and Dan Broderick had met at a dance in 1965 at the University of Notre Dame in Indiana. He was a 21-year-old medical student, and she was 17, about to embark on her own

REVENGE AND RETRIBUTION

college career. It was, it would seem, love at first sight. They married in 1969 and had their first child, Kim, in 1970. Four more children followed – another daughter and then three sons, one of whom died in childbirth.

Despite this, to onlookers, theirs seemed a perfect marriage. Dan had decided to combine his medical degree with a legal one, and Betty supported the family for a number of years while he studied, working as a teaching assistant, a babysitter and selling Tupperware and Avon products while raising the children. They also kept up a healthy social life – a society columnist from the *San Diego Union-Tribune* said, "They both were almost central casting for early yuppie."

All of that changed in 1982 when Dan, 38 years old and now earning over a million dollars a year with his law firm, hired 21-year-old former flight attendant Linda Kolkena as an office assistant. Betty immediately suspected an affair, which Dan denied, but their "perfect" marriage began to fall apart. When he finally confessed to the affair, Betty burned all his clothes and threw a stereo at him. He moved out, and what followed was one of the most bitter divorce cases in San Diego history.

Betty claimed her husband made it impossible for her to find a lawyer to represent her, so she broke into his home, spray-painted his bedroom and smeared food all over his kitchen. His legal contacts also smoothed the way for him to gain custody of their children, whom she had raised while he studied, so she took her revenge by ramming her car into Dan's front door, leaving obscene messages on his answering machine and defacing court documents. She wrote "God" in the space where his name should have been. She also, more than once, threatened to kill him.

Dan, who married Linda in 1989, had Betty arrested and briefly sent to a mental hospital. He also took out a restraining order against her and started to withhold support payments. If the threats continued, he informed her, he would have her jailed again. As case after case went her ex-husband's way, she came to realize one thing about the courts – she knew she couldn't win, she said.

According to her testimony, she didn't know she was going to kill Dan and Linda until the last moment. She said she had just bought about $400 worth of groceries, fresh veal and swordfish and, in her words, "all this wonderful stuff."

On the Saturday night she couldn't sleep. Just before dawn she got in her car and started to drive. She said she didn't know where she was going – perhaps down to the 7-Eleven at La Jolla Shores to get a half chocolate-half coffee and go for a walk on the beach, like she did some mornings. But she went to Dan's house.

Claiming she had found her daughter's keys to the house behind a chair in her own home, she told the court that she still didn't know what she planned as she opened the door. She climbed the stairs to their bedroom, and said she was surprised it was so dark given that the sun was already up. She took aim and fired her five bullets, watched in horror as Dan crawled towards the phone, took it away from him and left.

She turned herself into the police later that day. Her case quickly became a lightning rod for many aggrieved women who had suffered at the hands of partners – she had supported him when he was poor, and as soon as he had become rich, he dumped her for a younger woman, bought himself a mansion, and even a red sports car. She described what he had done to her as a white-collar way of beating her up. He had taken her kids, her home and her money.

After the killings, she was angry that Dan and Linda were seen as victims, saying she and the kids were the real victims.

REVENGE AND RETRIBUTION

One juror at the first trial apparently asked why she had taken so long to kill Dan under such extreme provocation.

That trial ended up as a mistrial, after two of the jurors argued that the charge should be manslaughter rather than murder, as they believed there was no planning or intent, leaving the jury hung. A second trial was held, and her story changed – she now claimed she had actually intended to kill herself in front of the couple but had been startled when Linda yelled out, "Call the police!" This change of story was incriminating, as was a tape of a phone call found by police on which she was heard to say she wished Dan would die.

Betty Broderick was sentenced to two consecutive terms of 15 years to life plus two years for illegal use of a firearm, the maximum under the law. In jail she wrote a book telling her personal story of the marriage, the divorce and the murder – it is called *Telling on Myself*.

AILEEN WUORNOS – MONSTER

The film was called *Monster*, and it would mean a Best Actress Oscar for Charlize Theron – her transformation from Hollywood beauty to the serial killer Aileen Wuornos astonishing fans and critics alike. Her portrayal of Wuornos was terrifying and remarkable. But not as terrifying and remarkable as the woman herself.

Wuornos was born in 1956. Her father had been convicted of child molestation and later killed himself in prison. Her mother then abandoned her, and she went to live with her grandparents – but her grandfather beat her, and her grandmother was an alcoholic. By the time she was 11, she was trading sexual acts for food, cigarettes and drugs. Pregnant at 14, she gave the baby up for adoption, and then her grandparents kicked her out. She soon turned to prostitution and petty crime. Between the ages of 14 and 22, she attempted suicide six times.

In 1976, she hitchhiked to Florida, where she lived for the rest of her life. She became well known to law enforcement and was described as erratic and easily angered. It was this anger that was to spill over into a series of crimes that would

REVENGE AND RETRIBUTION

make her famous. She was out to take revenge on the world for what it had done to her – men especially.

She claimed her first victim had beaten and raped her, and it later turned out that 51-year-old electronics store owner Richard Mallory had one prior conviction for sexual assault. Wuornos was no stranger to sexual violence, but it seems something about Mallory pushed her over the edge. She shot him three times. His body was found in the woods on 13 December 1989.

Six months later, the body of 47-year-old construction worker David Spears was found along US Route 19 in Florida. He was naked and had been shot six times with a .22 gun – the same gun that was then used to shoot part-time rodeo worker Charles Carskaddon, whose decomposing body was found wrapped in a blanket on 6 June 1990. Witnesses had seen Wuornos driving Carskaddon's car, and she also pawned a gun belonging to him soon after he went missing.

A month later, 65-year-old Peter Siems went missing, never to be found. But his car was, with Wuornos's handprints all over it.

Her fifth known killing was 50-year-old Troy Burress. His body was found dumped beside State Road 19 in Marion County on 4 August 1990, with two gunshot wounds. A month later, the body of Charles Richard "Dick" Humphreys, a former child-abuse investigator and chief of police, was found. It is not known if Wuornos was aware of whom she was killing, but she shot him seven times in the head and body. His car was found a week later, miles away.

Wuornos's final victim was also a policeman, Walter Antonio. His naked body was found on a logging road, with four bullet holes in it. Again his car had been taken, again it was found far from the body.

Were these random killings? Were they men who had solicited her? Was it about getting the cars? And did she act alone?

In 1986, Wuornos had met 24-year-old Tyria Jolene Moore, six years her junior. Witnesses questioned about the disappearance of Peter Siems mentioned seeing two women in the vicinity. Did Moore also participate in the killings?

Moore was tracked down and arrested. She agreed to help make Wuornos confess in return for immunity from conviction. In a series of phone calls, Moore convinced Wuornos to take full responsibility for the murders. Wuornos said that in each case she had acted in self-defence, after the men had tried to rape her. Wuornos would later modify her statement to say that Richard Mallory had actually raped her, but the others had not, although they had tried.

Whether this was true or not, Wuornos received six death sentences – the seventh body, that of Peter Siems, was never found, so no murder conviction was ever registered. It was not needed. Her sentence was death.

She spent ten years on death row, waiving any attempts for clemency. She didn't try and appeal her death sentence, as she said she would kill again, because she had hate crawling through her system.

Instead of a final meal, she had a cup of coffee, and was then given a lethal injection, on 9 October 2002. She told the prison officer who was with her at the end that she would return, like Independence Day with Jesus. What she meant, if anything, is a mystery.

BRENDA ANN SPENCER – I DON'T LIKE MONDAYS

"It was the perfect senseless act and this was the perfect senseless reason for doing it. So perhaps I wrote the perfect senseless song to illustrate it." – Bob Geldof

Long before Live Aid, Bob Geldof was best known as the lead singer and songwriter of the Boomtown Rats, and they were best known for one song: "I Don't Like Mondays". It was number one in the UK in 1979 for four weeks. The band had been in Atlanta, Georgia in the US, doing a radio interview on 29 January, when a telex had come into the station. There had been a shooting at Cleveland Elementary School in San Diego, California. Two adults were dead, and eight children and one police officer wounded.

The telex said that the shooter had been captured and was a female teenager. A reporter had managed to call her at her house before she was arrested and asked her why she did it. Her reply was slightly longer that what Bob Geldof would use. She not only said she didn't like Mondays, she also said that what she did had livened up her day.

It was not the first ever school shooting in the US, but it would set the pattern for the epidemic to follow. While it is traditional in most cases to say that no one would have believed that the shooter would do such a thing, no one ever said that about 16-year-old Brenda Ann Spencer, the shooter at Cleveland Elementary. Geldof's line about her daddy not understanding, because she was always good as gold, was definitely poetic licence.

Spencer was born in San Diego on 3 April 1962. Her parents had divorced when she was nine, and she lived with her father Wallace, a gun enthusiast. Living in extreme poverty, they slept on a single mattress together in a house covered in alcohol bottles. Spencer claimed her father abused her; he denied it.

She attended Patrick Henry High School but was often absent and often fell asleep in class. Other students described being scared of her. One of her hobbies was to shoot birds, and she was known as a thief, who referred to the police as "pigs". She also told classmates that one day she would do something big to get on TV.

In December 1978, she was recommended to be placed in a mental hospital for depression. Her father refused and for Christmas that year gave her a Ruger 10/22 semi-automatic .22 rifle with telescopic sight and 500 rounds of ammunition. Asked later why her dad have given it to her, she said he bought the rifle so she would kill herself. But she had other plans for it.

Their house was just across the road from Cleveland Elementary. On 29 January 1979, students began to assemble outside the gates, waiting for the principal, 53-year-old Burton Wragg, to open them. Among them was nine-year-old Cam Miller. There was the sound of a shot and the nine-year-old collapsed. Later Spencer would say that she shot him first because he was wearing her favourite colour – blue.

REVENGE AND RETRIBUTION

In the next 20 minutes, Spencer fired 36 rounds. Eleven hit their mark. Principal Wragg was killed, as was 56-year-old school custodian Mike Suchar, who was trying to pull children to safety. Miraculously, no child died – Cam Miller could still show the scar on his chest 40 years later.

Also injured was a police officer, Robert Robb, who had rushed to the scene. As more police arrived, they commandeered a garbage truck and parked it between the house and the school, forming a barrier against the shots. Spencer fired a few more shots, then barricaded herself in the house.

The stand-off lasted for seven hours. It was during this time that the reporter from *The San Diego Union-Tribune* called her and got the immortal quote. She also told police that she planned to "come out shooting". In the end it was the offer of a meal from Burger King that drew Spencer out of the house.

Charged as an adult, on 4 April 1980, Spencer was found guilty, and sentenced to concurrent terms of 25 years and life in prison for the two deaths. Nine counts of attempted murder were dismissed.

At the trial and subsequent parole hearings, her defence lawyers continued to argue that this was a case of diminished responsibility caused by the abuse she suffered at the hands of her father. He always denied the abuse. But in a disturbing development, he later married one of Spencer's first cellmates – a 17-year-old who bore a striking resemblance to his daughter…

And did Spencer know about the song? Yes, apparently – Geldof revealed that she had written to him about it, saying that "she was glad she'd done it because I'd made her famous. Which is not a good thing to live with."

JODI ANN ARIAS – THE STALKER

We've all watched the scene, many of us peeking through our fingers. When Janet Leigh takes a shower at the Bates Motel, we know what's coming, in a way that those who saw *Psycho* when it first came out didn't. Alfred Hitchcock had deliberately kept anyone from knowing that 47 minutes into the film his heroine would be stabbed to death. So, for audiences back in 1960, the 45 seconds of the shower scene were even more horrifying.

How shocked was Travis Alexander when his ex-girlfriend Jodi Ann Arias pulled back the shower curtain and plunged a knife into him? Theirs had always been an intense and tumultuous relationship, even after they broke up, but can anything prepare you for such a violent end? And unlike Hitchcock's film, there were no jump cuts, no body doubles and no clever edits. Travis Alexander had to take every blow – all 27 of them.

They met in September 2006. Born in California in 1977, Alexander had held down various jobs – motivational speaker, retail salesperson, telemarketer. He was also a devout Mormon, had grown up with his paternal grandparents from the age of eight, and had settled in Mesa, Arizona, where he worked as a salesman of legal service products.

She was also from California, born in 1980 in Salinas, and had been an aspiring photographer before she got a job at the same legal services company as Alexander. It was at a work conference in Las Vegas, Nevada that they met, and the chemistry was instant. As a friend later told ABC news: "She was really excited about the relationship. She loved how funny he was, how much fun they would have together." Arias converted to the Church of Jesus Christ of Latter-day Saints on 26 November 2006 and moved to Mesa in February 2007. But she returned to California in April 2008, to live with her grandparents. The pair began a long-distance relationship, taking turns travelling back and forth from California and Arizona – a 16-hour drive.

Their relationship was fervent and impassioned, and as with many long-distance relationships, sometimes the strain would be too much and they separated. However, even if they were seeing other people, they continued to sext each other.

It was during this time that Alexander's friends began worrying about him. The behaviour of Arias seemed to be becoming more obsessive. "I started seeing things that were just disturbing," one friend said. "I said, 'Travis, I'm afraid we're gonna find you chopped up in her freezer...' From very early on, she was completely obsessed with him."

The friend added that her jealousy was obvious – when they went out: "She just had to sit right by him. She didn't appreciate it when he was talking to another female."

On 4 June 2008, Alexander had a conference call booked for the evening. As far as everyone knew, he was no longer seeing Arias. Phone records showed that, as he had told his friends, in May they had had a huge fight and had told each other they never wanted to see each other again. He told them he believed she had been stalking his Facebook and may have slashed his tyres. Alexander ironed his shirt and then went to take a shower.

His failure to turn up for the conference call was unusual – he was known as a reliable worker and had confirmed his participation not long before. Work colleagues hoped he was okay.

The next day, Arias left the body and went to a work conference in West Jordan, Utah, ten and a half hours north of Mesa. One fellow employee noticed that her blonde hair was now brown, and she had cuts on her hands, which she told him was from cutting her hand while working at a restaurant called Margaritaville, though it turned out that no such restaurant existed.

The next day she headed back home to California, another 12-hour drive. When she returned the rental car, it had travelled about 2,800 miles. The company noted that two floor mats were missing, and there were various red stains on the upholstery, but these were cleaned off immediately by staff before they could be analyzed.

On the drive, Arias had made several phone calls – to Trent Alexander. She left several voicemail messages for him – obviously trying to cover for the killing.

Alexander failed to turn up for work for several days, and on 9 June, friends went to his house to see if he was all right. What they found shocked them. In the hallway leading to the bathroom there were huge pools of blood. There was a bloody handprint outside the bedroom door. And in the shower was the body of Trent Alexander.

REVENGE AND RETRIBUTION

He had not only been stabbed 27 times, he had also had his jugular vein, carotid artery and trachea cut, and had been shot in the head. The friends called 911 and police and first responders arrived. They asked if the friends knew anyone who might have done this to Alexander. They did.

A search of the house also found a camera, which had been thrown into the washing machine. On it were pictures of Alexander and Arias having sex at 1.40 p.m. on the day of the murder, then at 5.29 p.m., pictures of them both in the shower. And finally, a few moments later, Alexander on the floor of the bathroom bleeding profusely. The DNA of Arias was found on the camera, as well as the handprint outside the bedroom door, as well as everywhere else.

She was arrested at home in California the same day. She initially denied visiting Alexander, but then admitted she had been there. She told them they had had sex and then she had taken pictures of them in the shower. Moments later, she said, masked intruders had broken in and attacked them, hence the cuts on her hands. The police didn't even pretend to believe her.

The trial began on 2 January 2013 – Arias pleaded not guilty. By now her story was that she killed Alexander in self-defence after he attacked her for dropping his new camera, but that she blacked out when trying to recall the stabbing.

During the trial, it was in fact revealed that Arias had taken a .25 gun – the same calibre as the one used on Alexander – from her grandparents' house, having staged a fake robbery to explain its disappearance. This showed that the murder was premeditated.

Arias was on the stand for 18 days – an unprecedented amount of time, as details of their relationship were explored in detail. A sex tape was played, on which Alexander described wanting to tie Arias to a tree and sodomize her, to which Arias responded that it was so debasing she liked it. She argued that he was abusive towards her, showing a bent finger she said he had broken. The defence also accused him of seeing multiple women while dating Arias and produced an email in which he wrote, "I am a bit of a sociopath." And as for being premeditated, if that was so, why would she spend the night before with him?

It was to no avail. On 8 May 2013, after 15 hours of deliberation, Arias was found guilty of first-degree murder.

Various battles then took place over whether she should face the death penalty or a life sentence. In the end it was the latter. She was also ordered to pay $32,000 to the Alexander family. Her own trials had cost the state of Arizona $3 million. But for their money, eager crime fans were in a ringside seat in a story as shocking as *Psycho*. As the *Toronto Star* put it: "With its mix of jealousy, religion, murder, and sex, the Jodi Arias case shows what happens when the justice system becomes entertainment."

SHI JIANQIAO – THE ASSASSIN

She had been born Shi Gulan, meaning "Valley Orchid", but for what she was about to do, a name like that didn't quite fit the bill. So she changed it to two Chinese characters, one meaning "sword" and the other "to raise". And thus, Shi Jianqiao prepared herself for an act of retribution that was to make her famous in China and around the world.

She was born in either 1904 or 1905, in the village of Shazigang in Anhui Province in East China. Her grandfather was a farmer, but her father, Shi Congbin, rose up to be a decorated soldier, as did his brother, Shi Jianqiao's uncle. By the time she was 20, her father was director of military affairs in Shandong Province under the local warlord Zhang Zongchang as part of the Fengtian clique. They fought frequent battles against a neighbouring clique, the Zhili.

In October 1925, Shi Jianqiao's father was surrounded by troops of the Zhili warlord Sun Chuanfang. He was killed, and his head was placed on a stake at the train station at Bengbu, Anhui, to be viewed by his compatriots.

In 1927, during the forced reunification of China, the era of warlords came to an end in many places. Sun Chuanfang was deposed, and he retired from the military, founding the Tianjin Qingxiu lay-Buddhist society. He could put his fighting days behind him. Or so he thought.

Little did he know, his movements were being watched. He may have forgotten the death and decapitation of Shi Congbin, as may have many of the former fighters in the wars, but one woman hadn't – Shi Jianqiao.

In 1935, she had moved to Tianjin and spent her days at the recitation hall where Sun Chuanfang held his services. She waited and watched, coming to know his movements better than he did.

On 13 November, he was leading a service, kneeling to recite a Buddhist sutra, when she approached him from behind. Everyone else at the temple had their eyes closed. Shi Jianqiao may have been a sword raiser, but her method of killing was more modern and pragmatic. From her kimono she took a Browning pistol, aimed, and shot her father's killer three times in the head.

The temple was in uproar, but Shi Jianqiao remained calm. She declared that she had avenged the murder of her father and that they should not fear her, as she would not hurt anyone else. Then she handed out mimeographed booklets explaining her motivation and apologizing for spilling blood in a temple. The booklets also contained poems she had written to her father, a photograph of her father in his school uniform and her will.

She was arrested, and the trial was a media sensation, the likes of which China had never seen. Reporters and photographers flocked from all over China, and she gave interviews from prison explaining how she had married a man shortly after her father's death, but he had proved unequal to the task of retribution, so she had divorced him and taken on the job

REVENGE AND RETRIBUTION

herself. In modern terms, she was saying if you want something done, give the job to a woman.

Twice she was convicted, twice she appealed. The case eventually made it up to the Supreme Court of China. The defence argued that she had a duty of filial piety to her father, to avenge his death. The prosecution argued that this was not filial piety, it was a cold-blooded murder – the idea that the death of Shi Congbin, a soldier killed on the field of battle, was in any way unjust was false. At the second appeal her sentence was reduced from ten to seven years.

Then in 1936, with public sentiment fully behind Shi Jianqiao, the government stepped in. Shi Jianqiao's "murderous behaviour", the government declared, "constitutes a violation of criminal law". However, they added, "her intent merits commiseration and the extraordinary circumstances [of the crime] are forgivable." She was granted a full pardon and released.

From 1949, Shi Jianqiao served in the Communist government until her death in 1979, at the age of 74, still loved by the public that had cheered her release 43 years earlier.

CLARA SUAREZ HARRIS – A SUDDEN PASSION?

She wanted, she said during the trial, to hurt him but not to kill him. When Clara Suarez Harris ran over her husband David outside the Hilton Hotel in Nassau Bay, Texas, the question was whether she had decided to murder her husband or not. But this was not the only question. Much of the case hinged on whether or not she had run into him one – or three – times.

Harris and her husband were both dentists and ran a hugely successful chain of offices, enabling them to buy an expensive house and a Mercedes-Benz. Married in 1992, they raised three children: two boys and David's daughter, Lindsey, from a previous marriage. Everything seemed to be perfect.

Then in 2003, Harris started to have suspicions about her husband and his former receptionist, Gail Bridges. She hired a private detective to shadow David, and it soon became clear that her suspicions were justified. The pair had arranged a secret rendezvous at the Hilton – and Harris decided to confront them in the foyer.

As Bridges told it, the moment they left the elevator, Harris leaped on them and "it all turned into massive turmoil, and the only thing that I could do was to yell for help... for someone

REVENGE AND RETRIBUTION

to please, please get her off of me." Staff came running, pulling them apart and ejecting Harris from the hotel.

But the ordeal was far from over. By the time the pair exited the hotel, Harris was behind the wheel of the Mercedes-Benz. She gunned it straight at the couple. "We were leaving the hotel and I was looking at David and I noticed all of a sudden his face changed," said Bridges. "And then I saw her."

Bridges was thrown clear, but David was hit at high speed. Bridges crawled over to David, who managed to speak to her before he died. "His last words to me were, 'I'm sorry, I'm so sorry' and then he lost his life shortly after that."

But according to her, Harris wasn't finished and came back to run over her husband twice more. She wasn't the only witness to make this claim. There was someone else in the car that morning – David's daughter, Clara Harris's stepdaughter, 16-year-old Lindsey.

Jumping from the car, Lindsey ran over to David and Gail, shouting, "She killed my dad! She killed my dad!"

In court, the issue of whether Harris had run David over once or three times was crucial to determining whether or not she was just acting in the heat of the moment. Both Lindsey and Gail Bridges claimed it had been three times. Lindsey testified against her stepmother, claiming she told her to stop the vehicle, but Harris had ignored her. Lindsey also told the court that she had tried to commit suicide four times since her father had been killed.

The defence attempted to show that the car could not have been turned around quickly enough in the amount of space in the car park, but police were able to show tyre marks consistent with Harris looping back to hit her husband again. And, in a final piece of irony, a video recording, taken by the private detective Harris had hired to tail her husband, revealed that she had hit him three times.

Against the advice of her lawyers, Clara Harris took the stand and gave details of the hell that David had allegedly put her through. He was, she said, impossible to please, and she had resorted to getting a personal trainer and undergoing plastic surgery in order to try and keep her husband. When she found out he was having an affair with the much younger Bridges, she had snapped.

If she was trying to win the sympathy of the jury, she didn't succeed. She was found guilty of second-degree murder and on Valentine's Day 2003 – which would have been their tenth wedding anniversary – she was sentenced to 20 years in prison. She spent her time in prison converting school textbooks into Braille. She was released on parole in 2017.

As for Gail Bridges, when asked at the time what she would say to Harris, she responded, "This was an unfortunate tragedy and it did not have to end this way." And David? "He once told me that he would like to spend the rest of his life with me, and he did," Bridges said.

DARYA NIKOLAYEVNA SALTYKOVA – THE RUSSIAN NOBLEWOMAN

Who is the most prolific female killer of all time? We know that between 1590 and 1610 the Hungarian countess Elizabeth Báthory is said to have killed up to 650 girls and women. And not only killed, but tortured them in increasingly sadistic ways. She burned them with hot irons, poured ice water over them and left them to freeze outside, or beat them to death over the course of several days. She even covered them in honey and watched insects eat their flesh, sewed their lips shut to watch them starve and bit chunks off their breasts and faces to watch them bleed to death.

Servant girls, daughters of the gentry – none were safe. Anyone might be taken to her home at Csejte Castle and be killed. She was known as the "Blood Countess", and after her conviction she was bricked up in an isolated room at Csejte Castle, where she remained until her death in 1614. But 650 seems a lot. Might the number of her crimes have been exaggerated?

Let's turn to Darya Nikolayevna Saltykova, who is said to have killed 138 victims between 1756 and 1762 – if not the most prolific female serial killer, this would at least make her the most rapid.

She was born in 1730, part of a noble and ancient Russian family. She married into another noble family, had two sons and was then widowed in 1755, at the age of 25, inheriting her husband's lands as well as a large number of serfs. Contemporaries described her as gloomy but nothing more than that. No murders yet.

But after the death of her husband, she met and fell in love with young and very handsome Nikolay Tyutchev. She soon found out that he was also involved in a love affair with a younger woman, and then that he had secretly married her. In her fury, she had his house burned down and sent her serfs to kill her former lover. Forewarned, he fled with his wife to his own estate in Moscow.

It was then that Darya Nikolayevna Saltykova changed from gloomy to murderous. She was out for revenge against men. At first, she just took out her anger by throwing logs at her serving girls if she disliked how they cleaned her house. This soon escalated, and she would beat, whip and torture young girls and women to death, revelling in her sadism. She hated all women, she said, especially those younger than her. She tortured children and pregnant women to death, breaking their bones as she did so. She did not kill men but killed the women they loved – one serf is said to have lost three wives in a row to her murderous rage.

Saltykova was well connected with powerful members of the royal court and it saw her protected for a while. But so vicious were her crimes, and so frequent, that action was finally taken. Relatives of the murdered women were able to bring a petition before Empress Catherine II, who had her arrested in 1762.

REVENGE AND RETRIBUTION

Over the next six years, Saltykova was kept in prison while a thorough investigation took place – there was a lot of evidence to get through – 138 murders leaves a lot of paperwork. She was unrepentant, sure that her noble standing would see her acquitted. She was wrong. Of the 138, she was officially found guilty of 38, which seemed plenty.

This presented the empress with a problem. The death sentence had been abolished in 1754 and no one had ever been accused of such heinous crimes, especially not a noblewoman. In the end it was decided she would spend her life locked in the basement of the Ivanovsky Convent.

But before that, the empress wanted to make a public example of Saltykova, as part of her crackdown on lawlessness. So, she ordered a "civic execution". Saltykova was beaten in public in the Red Square in Moscow and then chained on a platform for an hour in front of the crowd, with a sign which read: "This woman has tortured and murdered."

She spent the next 11 years alone in her basement under 24-hour guard, with a nun bringing her food. The room was windowless, so most of her time was spent in complete darkness. To eat she was allowed candlelight; after meals the candle was taken away. She was sometimes allowed out to hear church services in the distance, to remind her that she was excluded from salvation.

After 11 years, in 1779, she was transferred to a room with a window. From here she would spit at curious spectators and shove a stick at them while yelling abuse. She remained there for another 22 years, dying in 1801. At that moment her nobility was recalled, and she was buried with full honours in her family's mausoleum as other nobles wept at her loss.

STYLLOU CHRISTOFI – THE MOTHER-IN-LAW

It has to be said, Styllou Christofi was not new to this. In 1925, she had been charged with the murder of her mother-in-law in what appears to have been a revenge killing in the small village in Cyprus that her family had been part of for centuries. A letter written in 1924 gave details of what happened. Christofi had been charged with the duty of arranging an honour killing of the old woman – her husband's mother, for a murder she herself is said to have carried out in 1911.

According to the letter, Christofi, her sister and a neighbour broke into the house of the old woman and attacked her with whatever came to hand. That included burning pieces of wood, which they rammed down the unfortunate woman's throat.

Christofi was arrested and charged with murder but found not guilty. It is not clear whether she was innocent or whether there just wasn't enough evidence for a conviction. But there is another possibility – at the time, honour killings were still a part of Cypriot village life, and a blind eye might have been turned by authorities if the murder was felt to be justified. As the historian Philip Jones wrote, in Cyprus there were "levels of behaviour or resolutions that the wider world might consider

REVENGE AND RETRIBUTION

improper or unreasonable, but which to the village itself were seen as entirely acceptable." Given that the letter said that this murder was in vengeance for another one, could it be that Christofi was released on this basis? Whatever the case, for many years, the murder – and the letter – were lost to history.

Then in 1953, Christofi moved to Britain. Her son Stavros had emigrated 12 years earlier, married a German woman, Hella Bleicher, and had three children. He was working as a wine waiter at Café de Paris, a nightclub in London's West End, when his mother came to stay. She had not seen her son since he left Cyprus.

Christofi and her son's wife did not get along; they argued constantly. It seems she was particularly angry that the children were being brought up as English, with no acknowledgement of their Cypriot past. This included language – Christofi had no English, and the children had no Greek, nor did their parents plan to teach them any. Nor did Christofi plan to adapt to any English ways, however long she planned to stay.

One can imagine that for Hella, having her cranky mother-in-law move into their family home and try constantly to put her tuppence worth in on the upbringing of their children was a huge strain. She and Stavros eventually decided enough was enough – Christofi would have to return to Cyprus. Hella would take the children to Germany for a family visit, and while she was gone, Stavros would confront his mother and force her to go back home.

We don't know if Christofi got wind of the plan, or whether she was as determined to get rid of Hella as Hella was determined to get rid of her. What we do know is that on 29 July 1954, Stavros kissed his wife goodbye and headed off to work. He would never see her again.

It seems Christofi was still used to working with whatever came to hand, in this case a frying pan. As Hella went about her chores, Christofi hit her on the back of the head with the pan. Then, with the children sleeping upstairs, she strangled her daughter-in-law with a scarf and dragged her body out into the garden, poured paraffin on it and set it on fire. This was seen by a neighbour, who didn't deduce that it was a human body being burned.

At some point, Christofi had removed Hella's wedding ring. It seems unlikely she wanted to steal it – more likely is that this was a symbolic act, undoing the marriage vows. Hella would go to the next life without a band around her finger. The ring was later found in Christofi's bedroom.

The fire got out of control, and Christofi ran into the streets, saying with her limited English, "Please come. Fire burning. Children sleeping." She must have known that this would lead to her downfall, but perhaps she had no other option. Or perhaps she thought that, like 30 years earlier, this might be seen as a justified killing.

The fire brigade came and put out the fire. When they found the charred body of Hella, they called the police.

It was obvious that the woman had been strangled. There were also bloodstains in the kitchen, and rags soaked in paraffin. When the neighbour came forward to tell what he had seen, Christofi was immediately arrested and taken into custody.

As had happened back in Cyprus, she was charged with first-degree murder. Her defence was not a strong one – she said, "I wake up, smell burning, go downstairs. Hella burning. Throw water, touch her face. Not move. Run out, get help." She was able to give no explanation for how Hella came to be burning,

REVENGE AND RETRIBUTION

for the actions the neighbour had observed or why Hella's wedding ring was found in her bedroom.

There have been questions asked about the interrogation of Christofi – no translator was available despite her limited English, and the police in fact used Stavros to translate his mother's answers. It is impossible to say if his loyalties might have dictated his translations, or indeed where his loyalties lay – with his wife or with his mother.

In November 1954, Christofi was found guilty and sentenced to be hanged at Holloway Prison. The nation was gripped at the time by the trial of Ruth Ellis and as the hangman Albert Pierrepoint noted in his memoir, the case of Christofi garnered much less media attention, as the story of "a grey-haired and bewildered grandmother who spoke no English" would sell less papers than the story of the glamourous bottle-blonde nightclub owner Ellis.

And so, on 13 December 1954, Styllou Christofi became the second-to-last woman hanged in Britain, six months before Ellis met her end. She was buried in an unmarked grave at Holloway, as was the custom for those who had been executed.

CHARLOTTE CORDAY – VIVE LA RÉVOLUTION!

It is one of the most famous paintings in history. Jacques-Louis David's *The Death of Marat*, painted in 1793, depicted the French revolutionary leader after he had been assassinated in his bath. It was painted soon after the actual event, which took place on 13 July that year and which had shocked the new nation.

Marat had long been a target for assassins. The leaders of the French Revolution were used to plots against them. But when he granted an audience to a 25-year-old woman from a minor aristocratic family in Normandy, it is unlikely he believed it would be the last audience he would ever grant.

Charlotte Corday was described on her passport as "five feet and one inch... hair and eyebrows auburn, eyes grey, forehead high, mouth medium size, chin dimpled, and an oval face". Born in 1768, she was a supporter of the Revolution, but of the moderate faction. She held Marat responsible for the September Massacres of 1792, where nearly 2,000 "enemies of the revolution" were put to death.

Jean-Paul Marat was a journalist first and foremost and his newspaper periodical *L'Ami du peuple* ("The Friend of the People") gave voice to the most radical extremes of the

REVENGE AND RETRIBUTION

Revolution. He also suffered from a debilitating skin condition, only relieved by spending hours in the bath, where he would write his articles to appear the next day in the streets of Paris.

On 9 July, Corday left her home and travelled to Paris. There she bought a kitchen knife and spent three days in a hotel writing her *Adresse aux Français amis des lois et de la paix* (Address to the French, friends of Law and Peace), explaining why she had decided to kill Marat. France was in danger of slipping into civil war, she thought. Killing Marat would save the Republic.

Her plan was to do it in public, but on finding out that he no longer went out due to his health, she decided to visit him and pretend she had knowledge of a counter-revolutionary group in Normandy. At first, she was denied entry, but later in the evening he asked to see her. She entered his bathroom and named the imaginary dissidents in Normandy; he noted them and assured her that they would be guillotined. Would that be all? No, she said and drew the knife, plunging it into his heart. He shouted, "*Aidez-moi, ma chère amie!*" ("Help me, my dear friend!"). They were his last words.

Justice was swift in revolutionary France. She was arrested on the spot and tried on 16 July, being found guilty of murder. She would be guillotined on 17 July in the Place de Grève.

She was granted one last request and said she would like her portrait painted. This was allowed, and it was done by Jean-Jacques Hauer, who had already sketched her during the trial. When he had finished, she suggested a few minor changes, which he made.

On 17 July, she was led to the scaffold, wearing a red blouse to symbolize a traitor. A large crowd watched as she calmly ascended the steps and knelt to place her head in the guillotine. A light summer rain started to fall. And then, so did the blade.

SYLVIA SEEGRIST – UNHAPPY HALLOWEEN

At first shoppers thought it was a prank. It was 30 October, after all, and the shopping mall was full of Halloween decorations. Perhaps there were firecrackers being set off as part of the celebration? So no one bothered to run for cover when the first shots rang out in the parking lot. Besides, the shopping wasn't going to do itself.

It was 1985, and this was Springfield, Pennsylvania – a proud town of 20,000 residents, 12 miles southwest of Philadelphia. The mall was a social hub as much as a shopping venue. Families gathered there to eat and shop.

Sylvia Seegrist had been there earlier in the day doing her own Halloween shopping. Then she went to a fitness centre and did a workout, before dropping the shopping home. She might have stayed there, but instead something inside her cracked – something that had been close to cracking for a long, long time. She changed out of her clothes and into army fatigues, grabbed a .22 rifle she had recently purchased and headed back to the mall.

Seegrist's life had been a troubled one. When she was eight, her paternal grandfather had sexually abused her. At 16, she

REVENGE AND RETRIBUTION

was diagnosed with schizophrenia, being hospitalized a dozen times. Then at 18 she joined the army but was harassed about her sexuality. She was discharged after two months for her bizarre behaviour. People in her apartment building were scared of her, as she would play loud music, shout abuse and do strange things like raking leaves at night. She hated children and wanted to fight a guerilla war in Iran against the Muslims.

She was well known at the mall, often ranting at strangers and harassing them, for example telling them their clothes were too bright and it made her angry. She also talked about spree killings, always lamenting that the shooter had stopped or been killed.

Returning to the mall, she parked her Datsun B-120 and headed towards the entrance. Thirty yards away stood a man named Edward Seitz. Seegrist aimed and fired twice, missing him both times, then kept walking. In what was to be the first of several heroic acts that day, Seitz grabbed an ice pick and drove it into a tyre of the Datsun so she could not escape.

A third and fourth shot also missed, one aimed at a woman using an ATM, one a man at the mall's entrance. Seegrist continued forwards, towards the Magic Pan restaurant. Here she claimed her first victim, two-year-old Recife Cosmen, who was with his parents waiting to eat. Two other children also received injuries: a nine-year-old girl was shot in the right cheek and a ten-year-old received a chest wound. Then she entered the mall.

She started shooting shopfronts and hit the ceiling of a drugstore, just above the head of a cashier. A man named Earl Trout was standing in the walkway; she shot him three times, killing him instantly. She continued to fire randomly, missing as often as she hit. Four wounded people lay near one another.

Further on, one man shot behind the ear was bleeding badly. One woman had been shot twice in the stomach, another shot once in the back. Augusto Ferrara was shot dead – one of three who died.

For those in the mall the rampage seemed to last forever, but in fact it was all over in four minutes, when another piece of heroism brought it to an end.

John Laufer was a 24-year-old graduate student, and he and a friend were sitting on a bench, oblivious to what was happening elsewhere in the mall. Seegrist came around a corner and raised her gun at Laufer. He thought that she must have blanks in the chamber but still felt she should not be doing something so reckless. He grabbed the gun. "You picked the wrong person to fool with," he said. "I'm going to turn you in now." She told him that she had family problems and suffered from seizures.

Laufer took the gun and sat her down in a shoe store. He then went and got a security guard. The security guard put her down to the floor and handcuffed her. "Why did you do this? Why did you shoot these people?" the guard asked. She said it was because her family made her nervous.

In court she was aggressive, swearing at the judge, and told him everybody knew she was guilty so they should just kill her on the spot. Instead, after a trial that lasted eight days, and in which the jury took only nine hours to find her guilty, she was sentenced to three consecutive life sentences – one for each victim she killed – and seven consecutive ten-year terms – one for each victim she wounded. Declared insane, she was initially interned in a psychiatric speciality hospital before being moved to the State Correctional Institution in Muncy, Pennsylvania.

The case did aim a spotlight at gun laws, and at issues around care for the mentally ill. Until then, to purchase a

REVENGE AND RETRIBUTION

gun, the buyer only had to tick a box to say they had not spent time in a psychiatric institution – now there would be background checks. It was also revealed that Seegrist had spent a considerable amount of time trying to get help – she had in fact been to the pharmacy at the mall several times in the days leading up to the shooting, trying to get tranquilizers. New laws were brought in to stop – as Seegrist's mother put it – irrational people having to make rational health choices.

As for Seegrist, in 1991, after being stabilized by medication and treatment, she told an interviewer she hated that she had hurt people.

ALICE UDEN – TWO TO TANGO?

Every murder case is, in its own way, strange. As much as we would like motives to be clear and straightforward, they are often complicated – even the killer may have trouble disentangling them. In other cases, evidence contradicts itself, people contradict each other, and times and dates become muddled and incomprehensible.

And then there are cases like that of Alice Uden, where the more you read about it, the more confusing it becomes. Who killed whom? How and when? And what was it all for?

In 1976, 37-year-old Alice Prunty, mother of five children by three marriages, moved to Fremont County, Wyoming for a new beginning after the presumed death of her third husband, Ronald Holtz. Holtz had gone missing two years earlier.

In Wyoming she met Gerald Uden, who had also been married three times. The pair fell in love, and five months later they became each other's fourth spouse. Together they bought a farm and looked forward to a happy life together.

Three years later, in 1980, one of Gerald's ex-wives, Virginia Uden, moved back to the area with their two adopted sons, Richard, 11, and Reagan, ten. The situation appeared amicable, and the boys spent time with their father and his new wife Alice.

On 13 September, Claire Martin, mother of Virginia and grandmother of the boys, called the Fremont County Sheriff's Department to report that all three were missing. Gerald confirmed that the boys had been supposed to go bird hunting but never showed up.

A few days later, Virginia's car was found. The three were not in it, but there were bullets and bloodstains. Gerald was brought in for questioning, and on being told that Virginia's mother suspected him – she believed he was angry at demands for child support – Gerald was physically sick. Alice was also questioned, in order to check Gerald's alibi – she became very emotional during the questioning, almost fainting at one point.

While police suspicions about Gerald remained, without any bodies there was no crime, and he was released. In 1982, the couple moved away from the area, ground down by community suspicions. They aimed to start a new life 1,100 miles away in Chadwick, Missouri.

Twelve years passed. The bodies of Virginia, Richard and Reagan were never found. The case had been closed, and had long gone cold.

Then in 1994, a man named Todd Scott, one of Alice's sons, turned up at a police station. He couldn't, he said, live with his guilty conscience any longer. His mother had confessed to a murder. No, not the three who were missing. She had told him she had killed one of her husbands, Ronald Holtz.

"She just, out of the blue, told me how she got up one night, got a .22, and shot Ron in the head," Scott said. "I don't know why a mother would tell her children she killed somebody."

The marriage between Ronald and Alice had been a difficult one – he was a Vietnam veteran and was known to be violent. In 1974, she had filed for divorce, and he had – she had claimed at the time – walked out on her, never to be seen again. It was only years later that she had told her son what really happened – one night while he was sleeping she had shot her husband in the back of the head, placed his body in a barrel and then pushed it down a disused mineshaft. Now in 1994, Todd was passing on that information.

But again, without a body, no charges could be laid given that the evidence was second-hand and circumstantial. Alice was questioned – again she nearly fainted – but she told authorities she had simply told Todd the story as a cautionary tale. She was let go.

Then in April 2013, a body was found in a barrel in a Wyoming mineshaft. It had a single bullet hole in the back of its head. DNA testing in August confirmed it was the body of Ronald Holtz. So, in September 2013, Alice Uden, now 74 and in a wheelchair, was arrested and charged with first-degree murder.

At the trial, in May 2014, she claimed she had shot Holtz while trying to protect her two-year-old daughter from her husband when the little girl started to cry. Alice said Holtz threatened to kill the girl, and as she tried to restrain him, he had knocked her over near the mop closet, before going into the girl's bedroom. Alice said there was a gun in the closet – she grabbed it and shot him in the back of the head.

The jury didn't believe her. She was sentenced to life in prison for second-degree murder – she had done it, the jury believed, but it was not premeditated.

But Alice wasn't the only family member facing being sentenced to life behind bars. Now 72, Gerald had been away when Alice was arrested, and was under the impression that his wife had been taken into custody for the murder of Virginia and the two kids. He contacted authorities immediately and said he wanted to talk to them urgently. When they brought him in, he told them that Alice had not killed Virginia and his sons. He had. He then gave a detailed description of shooting all three, placing them in a barrel and throwing them in a river. Richard was standing beside the tailgate of the station wagon, he told them, and he shot him behind the ear. When Reagan saw what was happening, he ran, tripped and fell in the ditch. He then shot Reagan.

And yes, it was over child support.

On 1 November 2013, he received three life sentences for the murders of Virginia, Richard and Reagan.

But there was to be another twist. In 2019, Alice died after five years behind bars. Two days later, Gerald asked to see his lawyer. He wished to withdraw his confession. He had not killed Virginia and the kids. Alice had. He had taken the blame in order to spare her. The lawyer took his statement to the authorities. But there was a problem – there is no mechanism in Wyoming state law for a retrial based on a prisoner recanting a confession after the possible appeal period, unless they could argue there was coercion. They couldn't.

The closer you look, the more confusing it is. Did Alice Uden murder her new husband's ex-wife and adopted children in a fit of jealousy, or over the child support being demanded? Or did Gerald do it, thinking that having a homicidal wife would be a good way to pretend he didn't?

When it comes to murder, nothing is ever simple…

OLGA HEPNAROVÁ – ACTA NON VERBA

The letter arrived at the newspapers two days after the murders. In it, the killer said she was paying back her haters – *acta non verba*, it said, "deeds not words". She had decided to sentence all of society to death.

By then Olga Hepnarová was already behind bars, but she had no desire to deny her guilt or to find an alibi. Yes, she had sent the letters; yes, she had done the crime. Did she have any regrets? No, just that she had only killed eight people. She had wanted to kill as many people as possible.

It was around 1.30 p.m. on a summer's day in Prague, 10 July 1975. A group of about 25 elderly people were waiting at a tram stop. They probably didn't even notice the pickup truck at first, even though it was speeding. It wasn't until the last moment that it swerved off the road and ploughed into them.

It was carnage – bodies and blood were everywhere. Some people ran to the scene, others ran away. Some ran to the pickup truck, which had stopped a few metres down the road, slamming on its brakes as soon as it had gone through the crowd. Witnesses assumed the driver had lost control, and they ran to his or her assistance. But instead of a shocked driver

REVENGE AND RETRIBUTION

shaking in the cabin, they found a 22-year-old woman sitting calmly at the wheel smiling. She turned to them and spoke, letting them know that this was no accident – she had driven through the crowd deliberately, aiming to kill them.

In fact, Hepnarová had been planning to kill as many people as she could for months. She had considered various other methods – one idea had been to carry out a mass shooting in Wenceslas Square, in the centre of Prague. She abandoned the scheme as she was worried that she herself would be shot immediately – she wanted to see the damage she had done and know how many she had killed. A plan to bomb a train was also rejected given the technical difficulties. She decided driving a truck into a crowd was simple, effective and would allow her to enjoy the sight of the dead more readily.

On the morning of the killing, she rented a Praga RN truck from a local company. She drove it into the centre of the city. For nearly half an hour she circled the tram stop, waiting for more people to assemble. When there were enough, she moved up through the gears and hurtled towards it.

Olga Hepnarová had had a difficult life. She did well at school to begin with but gradually grew estranged from her classmates, teachers and family. At the age of 13, she attempted suicide and spent a year in a psychiatric hospital. Doctors identified a number of problematic behaviours – "apathy, insubordination, negativism, detachment, vomiting, and nicotine addiction". Her sexuality was also raised as being a problem, seeming as it did to include both sexes, which was frowned upon in Soviet Czechoslovakia.

Declared ready to reintegrate, she remained obsessed with hatred for her family and for society. She wrote to one of her psychiatrists saying that she hated people, and that they had mutilated her soul. Her "mutilated soul" decided to seek revenge.

As she sped towards the tram stop, that revenge was in sight. Nothing was in her way, she said. It was the right time to do it. Three people died immediately and three more died later the same day. A few days later two more died from their injuries, making a total of eight dead. Another 12 people were injured but survived. All her victims were aged between 60 and 79. She told police that she immediately felt a sense of release and satisfaction.

Hepnarová was found guilty of eight charges of murder and sentenced to death by short-drop hanging. Short-drop hanging is a method of execution that results in strangulation. The victim is placed on a trapdoor and a simple noose is placed around their neck. The trapdoor opens and they drop only a few inches. The aim is to make the victim suffer as much as possible in their final moments.

At her sentencing, Hepnarová said she was not afraid of death. But according to the executioner, when her time came to die on 12 March 1975, she "became hysterical, begged for her life, and lost control of her bodily functions as she was dragged kicking and screaming to the gallows." Society had taken its revenge, just as she had.

MADAME POPOVA – HUSBAND KILLER

It has never been easy to be a woman, and if you were one in the late nineteenth-century Russian peasant classes, you would have had it particularly rough. It wasn't a great time for anyone in the peasantry, with high rates of poverty and starvation – the Russian Revolution of 1917 didn't come out of nowhere. But to be the wife of a peasant was especially gruelling; a great many found themselves trapped in abusive relationships, beaten and treated not much better – or possibly even worse – than the livestock that the men farmed.

Enter Alexe Katherina Popova, commonly known as "Madame" Popova. A native of Samara in southwestern Russia, she was so distressed at the plight of the women around her, all more or less held captive by their husbands, that she volunteered a solution for anyone who wanted it. For a small fee, she would kill their husband for them. If they couldn't afford a fee, then she would do it for nothing.

She was eclectic in her methods – some she poisoned, some she stabbed, others she shot. As some would argue later, it was effectively a form of female liberation, and one that cut straight to the chase.

LADY KILLERS

She was in business for 30 years and claimed to have killed over 300 men, which would put her high on the list of most prolific killers, male or female. She was only caught when one wife came forward to the authorities because she felt guilty about what she had done. Some have noted that only one wife out of 300 in 30 years seems quite a telling level of regret...

On her 1909 arrest, Madame Popova admitted everything. She was proud to have liberated so many women, she said, boasting at the trial – she acted as her own defence lawyer – that she had freed unhappy wives from their tyrants. She had never, she pointed out, killed anyone who didn't deserve it – she had never killed a woman, for instance.

When she was sentenced to death, an angry mob of men stormed the court and tried to take her to be burned at the stake – an early form of pushback – but soldiers intervened. They wanted to kill her themselves, which they did by firing squad the same day.

LYDIA ECHEVARRÍA – THE SHOW MUST GO ON

They were one of Puerto Rico's most famous couples. Wife and husband team Lydia Echevarría and Luis Vigoreaux co-hosted prime-time shows together throughout the 1970s and early 1980s, and their off-screen chemistry was just as strong in front of the cameras. He had been a television producer for years; now with his attractive spouse he was a star in his own right, only outshone by the woman beside him on the screen. And then he had an affair. With an actress half the age of his wife. And it all went wrong.

There had already been pressures on the marriage behind the scenes. The success of the production company did not always translate into cash – television is a brutal and precarious business – and in 1979 the company went into bankruptcy. At the same time, the first rumours began to circulate in the press about Vigoreaux's affair with 26-year-old Nydia Castillo. Echevarría, who was in her fifties, quit their weekly show and filed for divorce. So far, so celebrity break-up.

But on 17 January 1983, the day before the divorce was to be finalized, Vigoreaux left a meeting with Echevarría and their lawyers, where they had been discussing final financial terms.

He got into his Mercedes-Benz and drove away. He would never be seen alive again.

The next day, the Mercedes-Benz was found in a rural part of Puerto Rico. It had been torched. And inside the truck was the burned body of Luis Vigoreaux.

Such was Vigoreaux's celebrity that the whole nation went into mourning. At his funeral, hundreds of thousands lined the streets to bid him farewell, and thousands more attempted to get into the funeral itself.

Sharing their grief – front and centre – was Lydia Echevarría. She wept at his graveside, gave interviews about her loss and was said to once again capture the heart of the nation in her sorrow. She channelled her grief into returning to the stage – her first love. She also joined the cast of two long-running soap operas.

Then on 31 August, six months after the death of Vigoreaux, a newspaper reported that the police were poised to make an arrest. A "family of hoodlums" would be taken into custody, plus a well-known Puerto Rican female star who had masterminded the whole thing. The description of the star left little doubt as to who she was.

Sure enough, the next week, 64-year-old Pablo Guadalupe and his seven sons were taken into custody and charged with the murder – in three separate incidents – of a lawyer, another unidentified man and Luis Vigoreaux. Outside the court where they were charged, hundreds gathered, chanting "Murderers, murderers!"

The Guadalupe family was ready to speak, describing themselves as contract killers. Each murder had been at the request of an interested party. And in the case of Vigoreaux, the interested party was Lydia Echevarría.

REVENGE AND RETRIBUTION

Echevarría was arrested two weeks later and charged with murder, spending two days in custody before being released on the most expensive bail agreement in Puerto Rican history.

She was tried in 1986, and based on extensive evidence of her involvement, the jury took little time in finding her guilty. She was sentenced to 208 years in prison.

She had served 13 years when, in 1999, her health began to deteriorate. Echevarría counted among her friends numerous wealthy and influential people in business and the arts, who campaigned vigorously for her release. On 7 March 1996, the Puerto Rico Senate had voted 21–0 for her to be freed. Finally, in 2000, the governor of Puerto Rico commuted her sentence and she was allowed out, but under a strict curfew. She had to be home at 8 p.m. every night for the rest of her life.

Echevarría's declining health quickly righted itself and she returned to the stage in daytime performances. She also managed to star in a new television show, a prison drama called *Confinadas* (*Young Women Prisoners*). It was shot on location – at the very prison where Echevarría had been incarcerated. As people say, the show must go on.

FEMMES FATALES

And you thought they were only in films! Sure, many of the most famous ones are – Barbara Stanwyck in Double Indemnity, *Mary Astor in* The Maltese Falcon, *Kathleen Turner in* Body Heat, *Linda Fiorentino in* The Last Seduction *or Scarlett Johansson in the Marvel Comic movies. Cool and sexy women, as likely to shoot a man in the heart as to take him to bed – often doing both to the same guy.*

In real life, things can be messier. The women may not have classic film-star looks, but as Nobel Prize-winning author Alice Munro says, as long as they have the will to disturb, we are in their domain, whether they are slinky, sensuous and disastrously beautiful or not. But even if not, whatever they use to kill, the main weapon in their arsenal is desire. Seduction is their spider web: their victims crawl in, but they are never able to crawl back out.

Sometimes, like in the case of Penny Bjorkland, the desire they inspire is an unconscious reaction – her very appearance of innocence kept her safe from the law. But for others, like Ruth Ellis or Idoia López Riaño, their look is as much a part of their bag of tricks as any firearm. Draw the victim close, then strike. Ellis had her bottle-blonde hair done before each court appearance; López Riaño was known to reapply her lipstick between murders, even during them.

Sometimes they share their beds with heirs to thrones, as Marguerite Alibert did; sometimes their lovers are famous architects, like the husband of Alma Rattenbury. But anyone will do. More than one of the women in these pages has chosen an unlikely mate for their wiles, but that's not the important part. It is about the kill. And often making it look cool as you do it.

So – you can have your film stars, play-acting at seduction with other film stars, who are also just pretending. You can eat your popcorn, watch the credits and walk back into the real world. Just don't forget that out in that real world, there are other women who are not pretending. And who may well want you in their web.

MARGUERITE ALIBERT – THE PRINCE'S PARAMOUR

In the best-known photograph of her, her dark eyes stare at the camera with the classic head tilt of the coquette, long dark locks flowing down to her chest, the top of one breast held in her left hand, a ring on its pinkie finger, and a double string of pearls around her neck. Meet Marguerite Alibert, the Parisian socialite and courtesan who took the Prince of Wales – later Edward VIII – to her bed and was known the world over for her tempestuous relationships – and then for one of the most scandalous murders of the 1920s.

She was born in December 1890 to a coachman and a housekeeper, and her early life gave no indication of the heights to which she aspired, and then obtained. Brought up poor, she gave birth to a daughter at 16 and spent her late teens and early twenties living a nomadic life, hand to mouth. That all changed when she met Madame Denant, who ran a brothel in the heart of Paris. This was no whorehouse – the brothel catered to the tastes, and wallets – of the richest members of society and the aristocracy.

Alibert soon became one of Denant's most popular, sought-after and expensive employees, known for both her beauty

FEMMES FATALES

and her down-to-earth humour. Men were entranced, and out of bed they were keen to be seen with her on their arm. She became part of the Parisian demi-monde, those who combined both allure and a hint of danger, operating as they did at the fringes of society.

One man who fell for her completely was someone who was destined to cause his own scandal several years later. The then Prince of Wales would become Edward VIII, king of Britain, subsequently abdicating his throne for the love of the American divorcee Wallis Simpson. But in 1917, his relationship with Alibert presented its own threat to the royal family.

Edward was besotted with Alibert. The pair were known to drink champagne as he drove her around Paris in his Rolls-Royce. He also wrote to her incessantly – over 20 letters – signed with his royal "E" and calling her *"mon bébé"* (my baby). In the letters, he set forth not only his own feelings but chatted openly about other members of the royal family, those in the royal circle, and gave his candid opinions on military matters as they stood in World War One.

However, when Edward's affections were redirected to Freda Dudley Ward, a married woman back in Britain, he graciously asked for the letters back. Alibert graciously refused. He could have them, she wrote, in exchange for a substantial sum of cash. As he told an advisor, "Oh! Those bloody letters, and what a fool I was... I am afraid she's the £100,000 or nothing type... and she's not burnt one."

She was indeed the £100,000 – worth about £9 million today – or nothing type, but Edward got lucky. In 1922, Alibert met a new man – one whose wealth made £100,000 seem like peanuts – and dropped her blackmail threats. But if Edward got lucky, Alibert's new man got the opposite.

LADY KILLERS

His name was Ali Fahmy Bey – "Prince" Ali Fahmy – a multimillionaire from Egypt. Alibert converted to Islam, Fahmy gave her diamonds, they married in 1923 and a bright future was predicted.

It never came. The pair fought incessantly – they became known as the "Fighting Fahmys" – and there were rumours of domestic abuse on both sides. But it was to get worse.

In July 1923, they visited London, checking into the Savoy hotel. On the eighth night of their visit, they went to see an operetta – ironically, it was called *The Merry Widow* – before returning to the hotel. They had a late supper and then returned to their room.

The shots rang out at 2.30 a.m. – six of them. When porters burst into the room, Fahmy was sprawled dead on the carpet, four shots in his back, one in his neck and one in the back of his head. Alibert was holding a smoking .32 Browning pistol. She was arrested and spent the night in custody.

For the royal family, the incident was a possible disaster. Alibert still had Edward's letters, and if found guilty, she might release them to the press in revenge, causing a scandal of epic proportions. It was here that the power of the British establishment swung into operation, either naturally or through coercion. Fahmy was painted as a terrible foreigner – Egypt had become independent from Britain only a year earlier, so Egyptians were generally regarded as rebels and upstarts. Alibert was portrayed as a poor white woman who acted to protect herself from what the press called her "exotic husband".

Alibert was defended by Edward Marshall Hall, one of the more famous British lawyers of that era, who argued that Alibert had been the victim of bullying and violence, and that

Fahmy had once sworn on the Quran that he would kill her. As for the murder – "Producing a pistol before the jury," *The New York Times* reported, the lawyer depicted, "a terrified, desperate woman cowering before her brute husband." Alibert sobbed openly as she told of her ordeal. The prosecution was banned from mentioning her career as a courtesan, ensuring that the name of the Prince of Wales was never brought up as part of the evidence during the trial.

The jury took only an hour to acquit her, and the verdict was met with cheers in the courtroom. The reaction in Egypt was, it is fair to say, less positive.

On her release, Alibert moved into an apartment across the road from the Ritz, where she is said to have lived a quiet life until her death in 1971, at the age of 80. And the letters? She kept them until the end, either as insurance or for sentimental reasons – and on her death they were immediately destroyed. Any scandal had been averted.

RUTH ELLIS – THE BLONDE BOMBSHELL

She was a bottle-blonde 28-year-old nightclub hostess, he was a hard-drinking racing-car driver. This was London, it was the 1950s, and all hell was breaking loose. So, when blonde bombshell Ruth Ellis pumped three bullets into the body of David Blakely outside the Magdala Tavern in 1955, it seemed to capture something about the times.

Theirs had been an affair full of alcohol and violence. At her trial, she would note that she had recently had a miscarriage, which might have been because Blakely hit her in the stomach.

Ruth Ellis was born in Rhyl, Denbighshire, in Wales, on 9 October 1926, the fifth of six children of a cellist from Manchester named Arthur Hornby and a Belgian refugee named Bertha Goethals. The family moved to Hampshire during her childhood.

Arthur was abusive towards his children and impregnated Ruth's older sister, Muriel. He was questioned by police but released, and Muriel's son was brought up as one of the family children. Arthur's attempts at intercourse with Ruth were violently rebuffed.

FEMMES FATALES

The family moved to London. Ruth moved out and at 17 became pregnant by a married Canadian soldier named Clare Andrea McCallum. Ruth handed the child, known as Andy, on to her own mother.

At the end of the 1940s, she started working as a hostess and a nude model, and by the start of the 1950s she was working full time as an escort. Her bottle-blonde 1950s pin-up good looks made her popular with the clientele. She had an abortion in 1950. In 1951, she married George Ellis and they had a child – Georgia, whom her husband failed to acknowledge. She put Georgia into foster care, and the couple divorced.

For all the chaos and setbacks, Ruth was ambitious. She took elocution and etiquette lessons and rose from escort to manager at a nightclub in Knightsbridge – the Little Club, making her one of the youngest women in England to hold such a position. With it came money and celebrity friends. She even got a bit part in the 1951 film *Lady Godiva Rides Again*, which also featured Joan Collins' screen debut. It was then that Ruth met David Blakely.

Blakely was a racing driver, three years her junior. Within weeks he had moved in with Ruth, despite already being engaged. Ruth fell pregnant again but had a termination, as she didn't feel as attached to Blakely as he did to her. In fact, she had already taken up with another man, Desmond Cussen, a former Royal Air Force pilot and now accountant, and she left Blakely to move in with him in 1954. But the relationship between Ruth and Blakely continued, as did the violence – it was in 1955 that she miscarried, possibly due to his attack.

No one knows when Ruth decided enough was enough. But on Easter Sunday, 10 April 1955, she went to the house of Anthony and Carole Findlater, where she thought Blakely might be. As she arrived, his car drove off. He wasn't there, so she walked a quarter of a mile to his local pub, the Magdala Tavern in Hampstead, north London. Blakely's car was in the car park. She waited across the road, in the doorway of a newsagent.

At 9.30 p.m., Blakely left the pub with his friend Clive Gunnell and walked to his car. As he was taking out the keys, Ruth approached, holding a .38 Smith & Wesson revolver. She fired and missed. Blakely attempted to run, but a second shot hit him and he fell to the ground. Ruth then calmly stood above him and fired three more shots into his body at such close range his skin suffered burn marks. The bullets went through his intestines, liver, lung, aorta and trachea. A sixth shot jammed, and she finally fired it into the ground. Then she turned to Clive Gunnell and asked him quietly to call the police.

As she was arrested, Ruth remained calm. She spent the night at Hampstead police station and was ordered to be held on remand until the trial. Psychiatric tests were also ordered, but they found her sane.

On 20 June 1955, Ruth appeared at the Old Bailey. Dressed in a black jacket and skirt and a white blouse, her hair freshly bleached, she looked every part the 1950s pin-up.

When she took the stand, the prosecution had only one question – "When you fired the revolver at close range into the body of David Blakely, what did you intend to do?" The answer would determine if she faced the death penalty. She looked straight at the prosecutor and told him in a calm voice, that it was obvious that she intended to kill him. The jury took only 20 minutes to find her guilty, and the judge sentenced her to death.

FEMMES FATALES

Attempts were made on her behalf for clemency. Battles raged in Parliament about the sentence, while the American crime writer Raymond Chandler, visiting the UK at the time, wrote to a newspaper, calling the verdict a case of "the medieval savagery of the law". But Ruth herself made no appeal against the decision.

She did, however, reveal that the gun belonged to Desmond Cussen, and that he had taught her how to use it. The murder was thus premeditated, only increasing the appropriateness of the death sentence, according to the law.

At 9 a.m. on 13 July 1955, the hangman Albert Pierrepoint took her from her cell to a nearby room, where she was hanged – the last woman to be executed in Britain. She was buried in an unmarked grave within the walls of the prison. The night before her death she wrote a letter – to the family of David Blakely. She told them she had always loved their son, and always would.

JUDITH – THE KILLER, THE MUSE

It would be hard to say which is the greater painting: the one by Caravaggio, or the one by Artemisia Gentileschi? Caravaggio's, from 1598, uses his characteristic method of capturing the actual moment of the murder – an almost demure Judith looking slightly disgusted at the act she has to perform in beheading Holofernes, while her maid looks on beadily, with a sack at the ready to carry the head away.

But there is something about the Gentileschi, painted around 16 years later, between 1612 and 1613. Perhaps it is because the painter is a woman? Her Judith is the opposite of demure – her strong arms, one holding the head, the other thrusting the sword into his neck, show her to be more than a match for the strength of her quarry, while her maid seems equally powerful, helping to hold down the sprawled victim as the blood spurts. Gentileschi seems to have no truck with any nonsense that says women are the weaker sex.

The story is from the Old Testament's Book of Judith. The book tells the tale of the beautiful widow Judith, who is angered by her Jewish countrymen for not believing that God will save them from the Assyrian army, which is about to attack. Her attempts to rouse them into action fail. So, Judith rolls her sleeves up and gets on with it herself.

She and her maid go to the camp of the enemy general Holofernes, and she fools them into thinking she is a traitor, willing to give information on the Israelite army. That may be the case, but Holofernes also has other things on his mind – he desires Judith not only as a spy but as a lover.

He takes her into his tent and they drink together. Either Judith can hold her drink better than Holofernes or she tips hers out without him noticing because it is the great general who passes out. Seizing her chance, Judith grabs his sword and decapitates him with it. She delivers the head to her cowering countrymen who claim victory, as the Assyrians turn tail and run without their general.

Or as the Bible puts it: "Her beauty made his soul her captive, with a sword she cut off his head."

Judith came to represent the heroic spirit of the Jewish people and has since been featured many times in art and literature – not only painted by Caravaggio and Gentileschi, but by Donatello, Goya and Michelangelo, and her story has been set to music by Mozart and Vivaldi.

But it is still the Gentileschi that seems to capture her best. It is known that in 1611, when the painter was 17, she was raped by fellow artist Agostino Tassi, and we know that when the case was brought to trial, she was tortured with thumbscrews to test her honesty. We also know that Tassi was found guilty and sentenced to exile – but the sentence was never carried out. Might she have been thinking about Tassi as she painted it? Or maybe the whole damn patriarchy?

LADY KILLERS

After her victory, many men courted Judith, but she said no to all of them and remained unmarried and, they say, happy, for the rest of her days.

ALMA RATTENBURY – CHANGING TUNES

"Mr Francis Mawson Rattenbury, of Manor-road, Bournemouth, retired architect, who died on March 28, has left estate valued in England at £502." So read the small announcement in the *Derby Daily Telegraph* on 10 May 1935. An innocuous enough announcement, which few people would have bothered to read. But behind it lay a case that was to grip the entire nation and, indeed, the world.

In 1925, 58-year-old Francis had married 27-year-old Alma Pakenham in Canada. Both had been married before. A renowned architect, Francis had designed the magnificent British Columbia Parliament Buildings. He had in fact left his first wife, Florence, with whom he had two children, for Alma. Such was the scandal that the couple were forced to leave Canada and return to his native Britain.

Alma was a woman of considerable talents herself. Born in Toronto in 1897, she had a gift for music, playing as a soloist with the Toronto Symphony Orchestra by the time she was 17. The same year – 1914 – at the outbreak of the war, she married Caledon Dolling, a nephew of the Earl of Caledon, an Irish peer. He was to die in 1916 at the Battle of the Somme.

She spent the war years volunteering with various charitable organizations, then moved to London in 1918.

There she met Compton Pakenham, a journalist who would later become the bureau chief of *Newsweek* in Japan. He left his wife for Alma and they married in 1921, emigrating to the US and having a son. But the marriage foundered, and in 1922 she went back to Canada, taking their son. She worked as a songwriter and gave music lessons. Then she met Francis Rattenbury who – as men often seemed to – fell completely in love with her.

Back in England, they had a son together in 1928, and then Francis retired, at the age of 60. The marriage became more of a domestic arrangement than a passionate affair. They kept separate bedrooms, on separate floors of the house, with Rattenbury giving Alma £1,000 a year in expenses – around £8,000 in today's money, most of which it is said went on drinking.

He also offered to employ a live-in servant to help with the household chores and act as handyman and chauffeur. An advertisement appeared in the *Bournemouth Daily Echo* for a "Daily Willing Lad", and in September 1934, 17-year-old George Stoner moved into the house, turning 18 soon after.

It seems the lad was "daily willing" for more than just household duties. Quite when 37-year-old Alma and young George became lovers is unclear, although contemporary reports suggested that Rattenbury tolerated the situation – the house was too small for him not to have noticed.

Then on 24 March 1935, a local doctor received a phone call from Alma asking him to rush to the house. When he arrived, he was confronted by a "highly excited, incoherent, and intoxicated" Alma, who dragged him to the downstairs bedroom. There on the bed was an unconscious Rattenbury, with a blood-soaked sheet wrapped around his head and without his trousers. There was also blood all over the room. To add to the confusion, Alma had trodden on her husband's false teeth, which she said made her hysterical. The doctor called an ambulance to take Rattenbury to Strathallen Nursing Home and then called the police.

When they arrived, Alma was even more incoherent, but she managed to tell them that she had attacked her husband with a mallet. The doctor administered morphia to calm her down, and she was taken to the police station. Questioned in the morning, she told police she had not only done it deliberately, but that she would do so again. She then signed a confession, claiming that her husband was worried about money and had asked her to kill him.

Four days later, Rattenbury died of his injuries, and the police arrested Alma and George Stoner. Under questioning, Stoner said that it was he and not Alma who had struck Rattenbury with the mallet. As Alma had also confessed, both were charged with murder. By the time of their trial two months later, on 27 May 1935, both had changed their pleas to not guilty.

Given that the situation had been amicable until then, what had set off the chain of events? The prosecution argued that Stoner had gradually become more jealous and possessive of Alma. They also revealed that on 24 March – the day of the murder, he had visited his grandparents and borrowed the wooden mallet, telling them he needed it to erect a screen in the Rattenbury garden.

The prosecution presented evidence that Alma and Stoner had been on a trip to London that week, and Rattenbury had been left feeling depressed. When they returned, Alma suggested that Rattenbury and she go on a trip to Bridport. When she told Stoner it would involve them sharing a bed, he became incensed. The prosecution argued that he had therefore acted alone, and that Alma had tried to cover for him. In backing up this version, Alma defended herself with eloquence, while Stoner refused to say anything other than answer to his name. An attempt by the defence to say that Stoner had taken cocaine on the night and been driven mad failed when he could not identify what cocaine looked like.

Strongly directed by the judge, the jury found Stoner guilty and Alma innocent. She was supported half-fainting from the dock, while Stoner was sentenced to death. It was not a popular decision with the public, who had been following the trial avidly and saw a young man led astray by an older woman, who had been married three times – "a cynical woman of the world, taking her pleasures where she could find them" as *The Daily Mail* put it. When Alma left the court, she was booed and had abuse hurled at her.

What happened next makes the case only more tragic. A few days later, believing Stoner was to be hanged, Alma bought a knife, returned to Bournemouth and walked across the meadows to Three Arches railway bridge, which spans the River Avon. Atop the bridge, she wrote a note and then took the knife and plunged it into her chest six times. The note said that if she thought it would help Stoner, she would stay, but it had been pointed out too vividly that she could not. This, she wrote, was her death sentence.

What she didn't know was that a petition had already been started on behalf of "poor led astray Stoner". It gathered an astonishing 320,000 signatures, and on receiving it, the Home Secretary used his power to commute the sentence to life imprisonment. In the end, Stoner served only seven years, and on release in 1942 he joined the army, then lived a full life to the age of 83, when he died, on 24 March 2000 – the 65th anniversary of Rattenbury's murder.

PENNY BJORKLAND – THE FRECKLE-FACED KILLER

Sometimes what you are looking for will turn up in the most unlikely of places. In 1959, police spent two months looking for the killer of August Norry, a 28-year-old gardener, whose body was found in the hills above Daly City in California on 2 February, and whose car was found a few miles away, the seats covered in blood. The murder seemed a particularly brutal one – Norry had been shot 18 times. Whoever had done it really wanted him dead.

Norry was known to have been something of a ladies' man when younger, but in 1959 he was married and looking forward to the birth of his first child. He had no criminal record, and the police investigation turned up nothing in his life that could lead to such a horrific killing.

The only real lead they had was the bullets they recovered from the body. The .38 slugs were unusual, and traced back to a manufacturer in Connecticut. Only 10,000 were in circulation, and only a handful had been sold in the area.

One local who had some of the bullets was a 23-year-old gun collector named Lawrence Schultze. He had sold a box of 50 of them to a local girl, Penny Bjorkland, and they had done some target practice. Bjorkland was known as a quiet and shy girl, a bit of a nail-biter, but also in many ways just an average teenager. Blonde hair, blue eyes, freckles and a ponytail – "you know the type," Schultze told the police.

One part of Schultze's story caught the attention of the police – they had questioned a local boy who said he had seen a blonde freckle-faced teenage girl driving Norry's car away from the hills at high speed. This had been dismissed as too ridiculous, and yet here was the freckle-faced teen again, and her name was Penny Bjorkland.

On 15 April, the police turned up at the Bjorkland house. The 18 year old was sitting on the porch, calmly chewing gum. She spoke quietly as she was booked, and was taken to San Mateo County Jail. Then she told them why she had shot August Norry 18 times.

She said she hadn't planned anything, she'd just gone out that morning with a handgun tucked into the waistband of her trousers. One thing she could say was that for about a year and a half she'd had the urge to kill someone. She wanted to know if a person could do that and not worry about police looking for them and have it on their conscience. She had sometimes gone out with the gun and pointed it at trees, pretending they were humans and shooting them.

On 2 February, she'd been wandering around when Norry asked her if she wanted a lift. Both being part of a small rural community, they knew each other, and he had given her lifts in the past. It was then she decided what to do with her day.

As she got out of the car she shot him five times through the open passenger-side window. Then she went round to the driver's side, opened the door and shot him another five times. As she put it in her confession, she had an overpowering urge to shoot him, so she kept shooting, emptying her gun, and reloading. At some point she drove the car 50 metres, then dragged the body out. Then she shot him another eight times, got back in the car and drove away.

The police were stunned. The killer's lack of remorse, in fact her obvious satisfaction with what she had done, was baffling. "Who did you want to kill?" she was asked. "Anybody," she answered.

Interviewed in prison, she said she did have a feeling of animosity against her parents for something unspecified they had done five years earlier. She said she hated her family, and was going to sit in court hating them. She wasn't immoral, she said, but something immoral had made her pull the trigger. She ended by asking them to let her know if anything she had done got in the papers.

It did. At the trial, various battles were fought about her mental capacity, with defence lawyers attempting an insanity defence. But Bjorkland was no help to them, consistently asserting that she had made a choice and took responsibility for it. She was sentenced to life in prison, with no possibility of parole for seven years.

For the first time, she herself was stunned and upset. It was, she said, not what she expected, and it made her unhappy.

In prison, she convinced the doctors that she was, in fact, insane, but when she was transferred to an asylum, she cheerfully told staff she had been faking it. The director of the facility said, "She was quite convinced that once we had found her sane we would let her go free."

She wasn't set free. To her dismay, she returned to prison, where she stayed until the mid-1960s, before being granted parole and disappearing.

FEMMES FATALES

So, had she proved that a person could commit such a crime and not have it on her conscience? She told police that yes, she had felt much better since she killed Norry.

WINNIE RUTH JUDD – THE TRUNK MURDERESS

They spent their nights playing cards and, as the newspapers put it, "entertaining local businessmen". For two of them, one of these card nights was to be their last night on earth.

It had started so well. Winnie Ruth Judd, known as Ruth, Agnes Anne LeRoi and Sarah Hedvig "Sammy" Samuelson became roommates after Judd took a job as a secretary at the Grunow Memorial Medical Center in Phoenix, Arizona, where LeRoi was an X-ray technician who already lived with Samuelson.

Ruth was the daughter of a Methodist minister and had been born in Indiana in 1905. At 17, she had married Dr William C. Judd, a World War One veteran, and moved to Mexico with him. Twenty years older than her, William was addicted to morphine and had trouble holding down work, so the couple often struggled for money. In 1930, after eight years of marriage, Ruth left and moved to Phoenix, although the couple remained in contact.

She quickly found work as a governess and also found romance – her striking good looks won the attention of lumber merchant John J. "Happy Jack" Halloran, who was known as something of a ladies' man. Like William, he was married, but the pair became lovers.

By early 1931, she was working at Grunow and had moved in with Agnes and Sammy. Ruth was 26, Agnes 27 and Sammy 24. At first the arrangement worked well, but soon tensions developed, and Judd moved to her own apartment not far away. The trio remained friends, however, and she would often visit her old place to play cards in the evening. On the night of 16 October 1931, she did just that.

At some point in the evening, an argument broke out between the three. No one will ever know what it was about, but it was most likely over Halloran, who was known to all three of them and may have cast his affections wider than just one. Perhaps this was the source of the earlier tensions?

What we do know is that Ruth was not going to take the situation lying down. From her handbag she pulled out a .25 handgun and shot both LeRoi and Samuelson. She also shot herself in the hand, perhaps to pretend self-defence.

But what she did next was even more horrifying. Two days after the murders, she boarded an overnight train from Phoenix to Los Angeles, California. Along with her handbag, she had two large trunks, which she placed in the luggage compartment. Baggage handler H. J. Mapes became suspicious of the trunks – there was a terrible smell coming from them, and they began oozing liquid. Believing that the luggage might contain smuggled deer meat, he called ahead to order that the trunks be held until they could be inspected.

When Ruth arrived at the station, she was asked to open the trunks but claimed not to have a key. Her brother was there waiting for her, and she was allowed to go with him, but she had to leave the trunks behind. The police were called and they forced open the locks of each trunk.

In one they found the body of Samuelson, and in the other the body of LeRoi. Samuelson had been dismembered, her head, torso and lower legs stuffed separately into the trunk. LeRoi was still in one piece. Both bodies had begun to decompose and leak.

A nationwide search began for the woman they were already calling the Trunk Murderess. But on 23 October, a week after the killings, Ruth turned herself in. She was held in custody until 19 January 1932, when she was tried for the murder of Agnes LeRoi, but not Hedvig Samuelson. No explanation for this was given, but it meant that the dismemberment of one of the bodies was never introduced into the testimony. This was to be a major omission, as police had important questions regarding how Samuelson had been cut to pieces – it seemed miraculous that a slight woman like Ruth could have done such a thing by herself, and it was noted that it was done not only using strength but great surgical skill. Was there an accomplice? Who? The court didn't ask.

Also unresolved was another strange aspect of the case. The mattress of each of the dead women was missing – one was later found miles away in a vacant lot, the other never turned up. Police believed that the women had been killed in bed – but the mattress that *was* found had no bloodstains.

On 8 February 1932, Winnie Ruth Judd was found guilty of the first-degree murder of LeRoi and sentenced to death. After various appeals, the sentence stood. However, a ten-day hearing in early 1933 diagnosed her as mentally incompetent, and instead of being hanged, on 24 April she was sent to an asylum in Arizona.

It was not to be the last of her "adventures" – mentally incompetent she may have been, but she was a brilliant escape artist, managing to get out of the facility six times between 1933 and 1963. The final time, she managed to make it to San Francisco, where, as "Marian Kane", she worked as a live-in maid for six years. It wasn't until 1969 that she was returned to the asylum.

But what of the possible accomplice? The main suspect was Jack Halloran. In January 1933, he too stood trial as an accomplice to murder, and Ruth was the star witness. She claimed the dead women had started an argument over Halloran and attacked her, and she had shot them in self-defence, shooting herself in the hand in the struggle. In a panic she went to Halloran and had him go with her to the apartment. On seeing the bodies, he had helped her get them into the trunks, needing to dismember Samuelson to do so.

The defence case was simple – Ruth was criminally insane, so her testimony was inadmissible. Also, if she had acted in self-defence as she claimed, then it wasn't a murder, so Halloran couldn't be an accomplice to one. The case was thrown out. Halloran died in Tucson in 1939.

In 1971, two years after being taken back to Arizona after her sixth escape, Judd was officially released, and, amazingly, went back to work for the same couple she had worked for before as a live-in maid in San Francisco. She died peacefully in her sleep on 23 October 1998, aged 93.

JOANNA DENNEHY – THE PETERBOROUGH DITCH MURDERS

Joanna Dennehy "only" killed three men, and "only" stabbed two others. The three she killed she knew, the two she stabbed were strangers. Her aim was to kill nine men in total, like the legendary Bonnie Parker and Clyde Barrow had. She wanted, she said, her fun.

She said that she targeted men because she was a mother and didn't want to kill other women, especially not a woman with a child. But killing men, she said, could be good entertainment.

Born in 1982 in St Albans, England, she ran away from home at the age of 16 with her 21-year-old boyfriend John Treanor. On discovering she was pregnant at 17, she reacted with fury – she didn't want children – and on the birth of her daughter she started taking drugs and cutting herself. After a second child was born, Treanor left with the children, fearing for their safety.

Dennehy moved to Peterborough in Cambridgeshire, where she met Gary "Stretch" Richards and allegedly funded her drug addiction through sex work. Arrested in 2012, the 29 year old was diagnosed with antisocial disorder and obsessive-compulsive disorder. She spent some time in care but was released.

A year later, she would embark on her killing spree, in Peterborough near Cambridge. First to die was 31-year-old Lukasz Slaboszewski. On 19 March 2013, he and Dennehy spent an afternoon drinking together, then she took him home, promising sex. There, she blindfolded him and stabbed him in the heart, before throwing his body in a dumpster. Ten days later, she killed one of her housemates, 56-year-old John Chapman.

Then, hours later, she killed her landlord, 48-year-old Kevin Lee. The pair had been having an affair, and before killing him she had convinced him to put on one of her black sequinned dresses. He was wearing the dress as she plunged the knife into him.

All three were stabbed in the heart. The second and third bodies were dumped in a ditch, and the murders became known as the "Peterborough Ditch Murders". Dennehy later told a psychiatrist that she had found murder to be "moreish" and that after the first killing she "got a taste for it".

After the third murder, she wanted to taste it again. She convinced Stretch Richards to drive her to Hereford in the west of England. There she stabbed two men – John Rogers and Robin Bereza, chosen separately and at random. She stabbed Bereza in the shoulder and chest, but Rogers she stabbed 40 times. Both miraculously survived and gave evidence at the trial.

Forty-eight hours after she attacked Rogers and Bereza, the police tracked her down. Kevin Lee's body had been found, and his involvement with Dennehy as landlord and lover made her the prime suspect. She seemed to find her arrest funny, laughing and joking as she was taken in and flirting with the male police officers. Bail was denied – she would remain in custody until her trial.

While she was awaiting trial, police found detailed escape plans in her cell. She planned to cut off the finger of a guard and use the fingerprint to get through the security system.

In November 2013, Dennehy pleaded guilty to all three murders and two further attempted murders. During her trial, she told the judge she didn't want to be controlled by anyone – not the lawyers, not the police, not anyone. In response, the judge called her a "cruel, calculating, selfish and manipulative serial killer."

She became only the third woman in British history, after Myra Hindley and Rose West, to receive a "whole life order": life imprisonment with no possibility of parole. In prison, she continued to add to her notorious reputation. In 2018, she applied to marry her cellmate, Hayley Palmer, who was serving a 16-year sentence for robbery. When Palmer's family objected, the pair tried to kill themselves in a suicide pact. On her release in 2018, Palmer said she still planned to marry Dennehy, who had written to her, that they were both psychopaths, and that they would travel down a dark and dangerous path together.

In a final twist, in 2019, Dennehy was transferred to Low Newton Prison, the same place where the serial killer Rose West was being held. Upon her arrival, she allegedly threatened to kill West, who was moved to another prison for her protection. As Dennehy's sister said after the trial: "She likes people to know she's the boss."

TONI JO HENRY – STAR-CROSSED LOVER

She was, according to the newspapers of the time, "arguably the most beautiful American ever put to death". If that is enough of a recommendation to be a femme fatale, then Toni Jo Henry qualifies. But it wasn't a man's love for her that saw her become the only woman ever placed in the Louisiana electric chair. It was *her* love for a man – her husband, Claude "Cowboy" Henry.

They met when she was 23, and her life until then had been anything but a fairy tale. She was born Annie Beatrice McQuiston in Shreveport, Louisiana, in 1916. Her mother died of tuberculosis when she was just six. She lived with her grandmother while her mother was ill, but when her mother died, she returned to the care of her abusive father and, soon after, a new stepmother.

At 13, she was working in a macaroni factory, but she was sacked by her boss when he found out there was tuberculosis in her family. Worse, her father beat her for losing the job. It was the final straw. She left home and changed her name to Toni Jo Hood. She gradually drifted into prostitution and started using alcohol and drugs, including cocaine.

Claude "Cowboy" Henry was a client of the brothel where she worked, and it was love at first sight. He'd been a prize fighter when he was younger, but when they met, he was down on his luck and taking any work he could find. He helped Toni Jo kick out of prostitution and drug addiction. She married her Cowboy on 25 November 1939, and it seemed that the happiness she had craved for so long had arrived.

The moment they got back from their honeymoon, Claude Henry received a telegram ordering him to appear in court in Texas on a shooting charge. He revealed to Toni Jo that he was out on bail for the killing of Arthur Sinclair, a former San Antonio police officer, but that it had been in self-defence. She believed him and tried to convince him they should go on the run. But he turned himself in. Toni Jo was devastated when he was sentenced to 50 years in the Texas State Penitentiary at Huntsville – the equivalent of life. She made a plan to get him out of there.

Her time at the brothel meant she had plenty of underworld contacts. One of them, Harold Burks, who was known as Arkinsaw or Arkie, was then AWOL from the army and had served time in the prison where Henry was held. He claimed a detailed knowledge of the place, and together they decided they could get Cowboy out.

The plan was to get hold of guns and ammunition, steal a car and then rob a bank to pay overheads for the jailbreak. The first part of the plan was simple – Toni Jo was able to convince two teenagers to break into a gun store and get them the weapons they needed. Then they headed for Burks' home town of Arkansas – where he said he knew of a bank that would be perfect to rob, hitchhiking from Texas.

Joseph P. Calloway was delivering a new Ford V8 Coupe to a friend when he saw the pair and offered them a ride. They drove onwards towards Jennings, Louisiana, where the car was to be delivered.

Toni Jo drew out her gun and pointed it at Calloway. She ordered him to drive into a quiet country road and park the car. Then all three got out, Calloway still at gunpoint. Toni Jo ordered him to undress – she needed the clothes for Henry when they sprang him from jail. They also took his watch and the money he had on him, $15. Then they made him get back in the trunk of the car and drove on to Arkansas. It all seemed to be going to plan.

But Toni Jo had changed her mind about what should be done with Calloway. He knew too much. She told Burks to pull over again. She went to the trunk of the car and made Calloway get out. She walked him across a country field towards some haystacks. Then she told him to get on his knees and say his prayers. The moment he said "Amen", she shot him in the head.

The pair continued on to Camden in Arkansas, where the bank was, and checked into a motel, posing as husband and wife. But Burks had been completely thrown by the killing of Calloway – he later told authorities he had never even planned to rob the bank, or to spring Claude Henry, let alone kill anyone. His own plan had been just to use Toni Jo to help him get back to Arkansas, where he was courting a girl.

So as Toni Jo slept, Burks gathered up as much of the money as he could, as well as Calloway's clothes, and got the hell out of there. If Toni Jo was crazy enough to kill a man in order to free Henry, who knew what else she was capable of? Might she kill him too once her husband was out of prison?

Toni Jo woke to find Burks gone. She used what money was left to get back to Shreveport on a bus and sought refuge with an aunt, Emma. Emma, whose brother was a police officer, was suspicious about her behaviour and called the station. One of her brother's colleagues came out to speak with Toni Jo.

She confessed to everything. She even handed the policeman the gun she had used to kill Calloway – only one bullet had been used, there were still five live rounds in it. At first, she refused to name her accomplice, but eventually she told them it was Burks. He was arrested a few days later, and both were charged with murder, to be tried separately.

The trial was big news – Toni Jo's looks (the press called her a "sultry brunette") and the sheer audacity of the plan made it great newspaper fodder. It only lasted two days, during which time Toni Jo changed her version of events and said that it was Burks who fired the fatal shot. The jury didn't believe her, and she was found guilty and sentenced to death by hanging.

At her appeal hearing, Burks himself testified against her. The verdict was again guilty, the sentence again death. On a technicality, a third trial took place in January 1942. For a third time she was sentenced to die – but now by electrocution, which had replaced hanging as Louisiana's method of execution during the course of her trials.

On 28 November 1942, she was taken to the basement of Calcasieu Parish courthouse wearing a plain black dress and black pumps, where she was placed in a portable electric chair. She cried as they shaved her head and was allowed to wear a brightly coloured scarf to hide her baldness. Did she have a final statement? She said, "I think not." She was strapped to the chair, a leather mask placed on her face, and 2,000 volts were put through her. She was declared dead at 12.12 p.m.

FEMMES FATALES

And Claude Henry? Four days before Toni Jo was executed, he escaped from prison in an attempt to see her one last time, but was recaptured almost immediately. Ill health saw him released on parole in 1945, but he was shot and killed by a café owner on 15 July that same year, after attempting to steal some money. The last day of his honeymoon with Toni Jo was the last time they saw each other.

In March 1943, Harold Burks was also executed – in the same electric chair that had been the final seat of Toni Jo Henry.

TRACEY WIGGINTON – LESBIAN VAMPIRE KILLER

The headline, and indeed the film title, wrote itself – *Lesbian Vampire Killer*. But this was no schlocky straight-to-video slasher film. This was a real-life murder, and it captured the Australian imagination in the late 1980s.

Tracey Wigginton was born in Rockhampton in Central Queensland in August 1965. Her parents divorced when she was young, and at three she went to live with her maternal grandparents, who brought her up as a devout Catholic. They died when she was 15, and she moved back in with her mother. However, her mother did not accept her sexuality, and she moved out again to live with a friend, Kaye Warry. It was during this time that her Catholicism lapsed, and she began to dabble in the occult, starting up correspondence with a woman in Adelaide, South Australia, who claimed to be a white witch.

Soon after, she met a woman named Sunshine, and the pair were "married" in a Hare Krishna wedding. Wigginton found work as a bouncer – she was six feet tall – and sought out a man to impregnate Sunshine so the couple could have a baby. This was done, but Sunshine had a miscarriage, and the pair went their separate ways.

FEMMES FATALES

It was when she moved to the city of Brisbane that her fascination with occultism found full expression. She got a tattoo of the Eye of Horus on the back of one hand and her zodiac sign Leo on the other; she also had tattoos of a black rose and of Merlin the magician. She filled her room with black magic icons and drew occult symbols on her walls – sometimes in animal blood.

This was not the only thing she did with animal blood. At her trial, she said she had long ago stopped eating solid food – she lived on pig and cow blood, which she would get from her local butcher. When the butcher could not provide any, she killed animals herself. Their blood was good, but not enough. She wanted to escalate things. She wanted to drink the blood of a human. She asked her lover, Lisa Ptaschinski, 24, if she would open her wrists for her to drink from, and Ptaschinski obliged as much as possible. But again, it wasn't enough. Twenty-four-year-old Wigginton needed to go a step further.

Brisbane, Friday, 20 October 1989: council worker Edward Baldock, a 47-year-old father of four, had been out drinking and playing darts with friends all evening. He left the pub and walked to look for a taxi. He was approached by a car containing four women – Wigginton, Ptaschinski and two other friends, Kim Jervis and Tracy Waugh, both aged 23.

Wigginton left the car and told the drunk Baldock that the four women were all sex workers and asked if he would like to go with them for some fun. He agreed and got in the car. For a while, he held Wigginton's hand. She presumed he was lonely, she later said. Then, being drunk, he fell asleep.

The four women drove him to the nearby Orleigh Park on Brisbane River. Waking him, they walked him down to the riverbank. They asked him to undress, which he did, folding his clothes neatly and placing his shoes on top. Jervis handed Wigginton a Ninja butterfly knife. While Ptaschinski talked to Baldock, Wigginton approached him from behind.

She stabbed him 27 times, first in the back, and then, pulling his head back, she stabbed him over and over in the neck. Baldock, she later said, had made a gargling sound so she knew the blood was coming out of his mouth. So brutal was the attack that he was virtually decapitated.

She told police later that she felt nothing as she stabbed Baldock and even relaxed and smoked a cigarette as she watched him die. The three other women returned to the car, to let Wigginton drink the blood of her victim. Fifteen minutes later she came back, according to Waugh, with her breath stinking of blood. She looked, Waugh said, "sick and pale, with vacant eyes like a zombie." When Baldock's body was discovered, it was evident that someone had pressed their fingers into his wounds.

It was only when she got home that Wigginton realized her bank card was missing. She returned to the places she had been, including the murder site, but could not find it. She decided if she couldn't, nobody could, and went home to bed. She hadn't looked in Baldock's shoe. The police did.

By the end of the day, all four women had been arrested. In the beginning, Wigginton protested her innocence, saying she couldn't even kill chickens, let alone a human being. The police also took a while to accept that a woman could have carried out such an attack. But Wigginton soon changed her plea. She had done it, she said, and gave a detailed description. Apart from her desire to drink human blood, there had been another motivation – it was so hard to become famous these days.

Pleading guilty, she was sentenced to life imprisonment, with a minimum of 13 years behind bars. Given her guilty plea, there was no trial. The other women had pleaded not guilty and so spent 14 days in court as the details of the horrific crime were recounted. Wigginton's girlfriend, Lisa Ptaschinski, also received a life sentence. Kim Jervis, who had supplied the knife, was found guilty of manslaughter and sentenced to 18 years, reduced to 12 on appeal. Tracy Waugh was found not guilty, having not actually participated in the killing.

In prison, other inmates were scared of Wigginton. One said, she was "not like the other girls... She would sit there for hours rolling marbles and grating her teeth... She's evil. She's a strange person in a world of her own." Despite this, she was released in 2012, after serving 21 years, and has not been heard of since.

She gave one interview in prison, to the Brisbane *Courier-Mail*, saying that murder was a terrifying experience, and nobody should have that power, but everyone does. She herself found that scary.

IDOIA LÓPEZ RIAÑO – THE REAL VILLANELLE

"Idoia was, above everything, a slave to her body and to her hair... I never met an ETA militant who was more vain than this woman." – Juan Manuel Soares

It was the hit new television series of 2018 – *Killing Eve* was fast, funny and furious, as it pitted MI6 undercover agent Eve Polastri, played by Sandra Oh, against the mysterious and beautiful Villanelle, an assassin and psychopath played by Jodie Comer, who becomes as obsessed with Eve as Eve is with her. Over four series, the two did battle, joined forces, then did battle again, in a comedy as black as Villanelle's heart.

But the screen Villanelle had nothing on the real one – a Basque woman named Idoia López Riaño, better known as La Tigressa – "The Tigress". When Luke Jennings wrote his *Killing Eve* books, it was The Tigress who he was turning into fiction. What attracted him to her as a writer? It was simple, Jennings said: "She was clearly a psychopath and completely, completely without empathy."

Born in San Sebastián in the Basque region of Spain, it is said that López Riaño dreamed of being a firefighter. But in her late teens, she and her then boyfriend José Ángel Aguirre joined a separatist group fighting for Basque independence – ETA. She said she was full of romantic and idealistic notions. The separatists wanted people who were committed to their cause, and she was.

The militant group was made up of freedom fighters, mostly men, who were not afraid to kill for their political beliefs. But they had never seen anything like The Tigress.

She was beautiful, and she knew it. With green eyes and flowing hair, she dressed exquisitely. It is said that she once missed a target because she was so entranced by her own reflection in a window. Her nickname came not only from the way she moved, but because of her legendary sexual prowess.

Her first kill was at the age of 20. In November 1984, her boyfriend Aguirre, his fellow ETA officer Ramón Zapirain and López Riaño, who was calling herself "Margarita", stole a car and drove to a restaurant in Irun. There, they confronted French citizen Joseph Couchot and accused him of being a member of GAL, the secret Spanish state antiterrorist group authorized to seek out and kill ETA members. Couchot didn't have a chance to respond before the trio cut him down in a hail of bullets. It is said she kept firing long after Couchot was dead, "finishing him off with a coup de grâce as he lay on the floor" as Paddy Woodworth put it in his book, *Dirty War, Clean Hands: ETA, the GAL and Spanish Democracy*. The Tigress had tasted blood, and she wanted more.

Over the next five months, having been elevated to the elite of the ETA assassins, she participated in 20 murders. This included the bombing of the Plaza República Dominicana in Madrid on 14 July 1986, which killed 12 people and injured another 32.

But bombs were less to her taste than one-to-one combat. She used her allure to take police officers to bed and then killed them afterwards. In fact, she said, it was all she could do not to kill them during sex.

For all her talents, eventually she started to become a nuisance. ETA was a highly disciplined organization, and one thing Idoia López Riaño was not was highly disciplined. Members tired of her indiscipline, such as when she failed to return home after an evening out clubbing when she was supposed to be on duty. She missed one operation because she broke a shoe and decided it was more important to get it mended than to bother showing up for her assignment. She also took time off for a seemingly endless number of pregnancy tests.

The Tigress got bored easily. Once, she was supposed to stay in a car and provide cover for a fellow militant as he came from behind a wall to fire on a car full of army officers. The Tigress couldn't stand to be caged. She sprayed the car with bullets herself, mostly missing, and the car drove away.

Once she even forgot to bring her gun to a mission, but she was unrepentant when hauled before her superior officer. She shrugged her shoulders and told them she forgot, end of story.

The other issue was her appearance. While it was useful in her killings by seduction, these were rare. More common were situations where the group had to be undercover, and having such a striking woman with them, dressed to the nines, was not helpful. A fellow militant said to *The New Yorker*, "It took 20 days of deliberations, 1,000 French francs for brown contact lenses, and countless meetings to convince her that she should alter her physical appearance because we had to go unnoticed," he said. "She could not move in Madrid because she would attract too much attention... None of us wanted to accompany her."

FEMMES FATALES

In the end, she was proving too much of a liability. She was sent into exile in Algeria, where she spent five years. In 1994, she moved to the south of France, where she was later arrested. Extradited to Spain, she was charged with 32 murders and sentenced to 2,000 years in jail, but the maximum any prisoner can serve under Spanish law is 30 years. She ended up serving 23 – one for every known victim, and was released in 2017. In prison she married twice. The Tigress still had claws.

MIMI WONG – THE QUEEN OF ALL BAR HOSTESSES

She was known as the queen of all bar hostesses in Singapore, and in 1966, there was a lot of competition. But with her dark eyes, good looks and perfect figure, Mimi Wong had all the men she wanted wrapped around her finger, and she wanted plenty.

No one looking at her then could have known that this petite and vivacious 27-year-old woman would be the first woman executed after Singapore gained its independence.

Brought up in poverty, she got married at the age of 17 to a street sweeper named Sim Woh Kum. They had their first son in 1958, and a second in 1962. The marriage was an unhappy one – Sim often gambled away their money, and Wong was violent towards her mild-mannered husband, often beating him and once leaving a scar on his forehead. Eventually, in 1963, she left, leaving Sim to bring up the children.

It was then that she became a bar hostess, rising quickly through the ranks. Sim, who was still in love with her then, later said that Wong used to taunt him by showing him all the new boyfriends she had.

One new boyfriend was a man she met in 1966. Hiroshi Watanabe was a mechanical engineer from Japan, who was working for his corporation in Singapore. Back in Japan he had a wife and three children, but he was unable to resist the charms of Mimi Wong – nor, it seems, could she resist his. The pair began an affair soon after meeting, but Watanabe continued to go back to Japan whenever he could to visit his family – an arrangement that made Wong jealous.

In 1967, she became pregnant by him and asked for money for an abortion. He told her that she was richer than him, so she could pay. She did, travelling to Penang to have it done. Their relationship became strained. Wong met a businessman from Hong Kong and left Watanabe for him. But the businessman left her when she again fell pregnant. She gave birth to a daughter and returned to Watanabe as his official mistress. Wealthier now, he gave her $200 per month out of his income to support her and the child. Then they moved in together.

Late in 1969, Watanabe could no longer bear the guilt and told his wife about Wong, but he promised not to leave her. Then he returned to Wong with the intention of breaking things off, but Wong let him know something bad would happen to him or his family if he did.

It was then that he made his fatal error. He asked her if it was best if everyone met up so they could straighten the whole thing out? Perhaps they could all come to some arrangement?

On 23 December 1969, Watanabe's wife, Ayako, arrived in Singapore with the three children. They went to Wong's house and they all drank tea together. Wong gave the children sweets. They called her Obasan ("aunt" in Japanese) and played with her daughter. To Watanabe all seemed to be going well. What he didn't know was that both women were seething with jealousy.

On New Year's Eve, Watanabe got drunk and admitted to Wong that his wife had once called her a "prostitute". Wong was enraged. All thoughts of coming to some "arrangement" were over. First thing the next day, she decided to call her ex-husband, Sim Woh Kum. Did he still love her? Then he had to do one thing for her – help her kill Ayako Watanabe. Did he love her enough to do that? Sim admitted he did.

Wong's chance came a week later. She and Watanabe had a meal together, and she asked him to stay the night. Watanabe said he had to go back to work in the evening and would be finishing late, before going back to his family. Wong realized that Ayako would be alone with the children all night. She called Sim.

They arrived at the house Watanabe had rented for his wife soon after. Sim was carrying a bucket and toilet cleaner, and Wong told Ayako that Watanabe had asked her to find someone to clean and repair their toilet. Ayako let them in and led them to the bathroom.

It was the screaming that woke the children. Nine-year-old Chieko ran from the bedroom to see what was happening, and there she saw Sim Woh Kum holding her mother, with a hand across her mouth, and Wong stabbing her again and again. Sim had thrown the toilet cleaner in Ayako's eyes, which were red and swollen.

Wong stopped and grabbed Chieko, but she broke free and ran to the bedroom. Wong and Sim didn't follow, but ran from the house. By the time Chieko had got back to her mother, Ayako was dead, and the floor was soaked in blood.

Watanabe returned to find his three children sobbing over the body of their dead mother. Hysterical, he asked Chieko what had happened. His daughter told him, and also told him who had done it – the aunty, Mimi Wong.

Wong and Sim were arrested the next day and charged with first-degree murder. In court they both claimed that the other was the mastermind, and that it was the other who had done the stabbing. Wong claimed that she had only intended to slap Ayako, but her ex-husband had been greedy. Sim claimed Wong was jealous of Ayako, and that she belonged to a notorious all-woman secret society known as the Red Butterfly gang.

Chieko was the key witness, and the nine-year-old gave a graphic description of everything that had happened. She had heard screams coming from the bathroom. "They were screams of pain from my mother... The man was pulling my mother's left hand and Obasan was pulling her right hand. I saw blood on my mother's chest. I cried and Obasan covered my mouth with her hand. I stopped crying and she released me."

The trial lasted 26 days, and both Wong and Sim were sentenced to death. Two appeals failed, and they were placed on death row, where Wong became notorious for going round naked, until she converted to Christianity. Thereafter, she spent her days reading the Bible and waiting for death.

It came on 27 July 1973. She asked to be hanged in the wedding dress she had married Sim in. Her wish was granted. Mimi Wong, 34, and Sim Woh Kum, 40, were buried next to each other.

BONNIE PARKER – SUICIDE SAL

It is the classic "romantic" American gangster story – the lovers who rob banks, shoot law enforcement and light a fire under all social niceties. More than a story, it has become a myth, and every myth needs a foundation tale. The foundation tale of this myth is the story of a woman named Bonnie Parker and a man named Clyde Barrow – "Public Enemies Number One", according to the FBI and the newspapers: Bonne and Clyde.

Their perfect romantic ending, gunned down in a hail of bullets together, unbowed and still in love, has provided the template for any number of films and songs, and for any number of young couples dreaming of going out in a blaze of glory.

Bonnie Parker was born in 1910 in Rowena, Texas, to a bricklayer father who died when she was four, and a seamstress mother. In her second year at high school, she met and married Roy Thornton, himself a bank robber who would die in a hail of bullets in 1937, during a prison escape. Bonnie was not even 16 when she married, and the marriage didn't last. They never divorced but went their separate ways. She found work as a waitress, but in a diary entry in 1929, when she was 18, she was already writing about how bored she was.

FEMMES FATALES

In the most likely version of the story, it was at a mutual friend's house that she met Clyde Barrow. He was the fifth of seven children from a poor farming family and had already had a number of brushes with the law – he had robbed some stores, cracked some safes and stolen cars. When they met, he was 20 and Bonnie 19. It was love at first sight.

But soon after, one of Clyde's earlier "indiscretions" came back to haunt him. He was sent to prison for stealing a car. He managed to escape with a weapon that Bonnie had smuggled in for him but was soon recaptured. While back in, he was assaulted by another inmate, whom he killed with an iron bar – his first murder, but far from his last. Another prisoner already serving a life sentence took the rap for him.

His time in prison had, everyone said, changed him. It gave him a loathing of prisons and law enforcement that would help fuel his crimes. A fellow inmate and later member of Clyde's "Barrow Gang", Ralph Fults, said that he saw him "change from a schoolboy to a rattlesnake". But Bonnie seemed as attached to the rattlesnake as she had been to the schoolboy.

She, Clyde and Fults teamed up and started to rob stores and gas stations. When Bonnie and Fults were captured, they both served time, which Bonnie spent writing poetry. Fults distanced himself from the pair on his release, starting a life of crime elsewhere.

Bonnie and Clyde, now joined by other outlaws, Raymond Hamilton and Ross Dyer, began a spree of robberies and murders that made national headlines. They only killed to steal, but they had a lot of stealing to do. Between April 1932 and January 1933, they killed five people, including one police officer who had approached them in a parking lot. He was the first of nine police the Barrow Gang would kill.

LADY KILLERS

Clyde's brother Buck now joined the gang, along with Buck's wife, Blanche. They found a good hideout in Joplin, Missouri, but their alcohol-fuelled nights and the sound of gunshots led neighbours to complain. A five-man posse was sent to investigate. The Barrow Gang came out firing, killing two of the officers, before speeding away in their cars. They had left behind not only guns but a poem Bonnie had written called "Suicide Sal", and a photograph of her smoking a cigar and holding a gun to her hip. In today's language, the photograph went viral. Bonnie and Clyde became front-page news.

The gang now went on a robbery spree, pursued by police, the FBI and the world's press. Buck Barrow was fatally wounded during a shoot-out on 29 July 1933, and Blanche was arrested. Bonnie and Clyde carried on alone. On 16 January 1934, they managed to break into Eastham prison, where Clyde had served his time, and release five prisoners, including gang member Hamilton, who was serving 362 years. Two guards were shot. The press had another front page.

On 1 April, Bonnie and Clyde shot and killed two police officers whose car they had accidentally encountered near Grapevine, Texas. On 13 April 1934, an FBI agent obtained information that placed Bonnie and Clyde in a remote area southwest of New Orleans, near the home of Henry Methvin, one of the inmates they had sprung from prison. It was learned that Bonnie and Clyde, with some of the Methvins, had staged a party at Black Lake, Louisiana, on the night of 21 May 1934, and were due to return to the area two days later.

Before dawn on 23 May, police officers from Louisiana and Texas concealed themselves in bushes along the highway. In the early daylight, Bonnie and Clyde appeared in an automobile and when they attempted to drive away, the officers opened fire.

FEMMES FATALES

When Faye Dunaway (as Bonnie) and Warren Beatty (as Clyde) are fired at in the final scene of *Bonnie and Clyde* – the 1967 film about the infamous pair, their bodies are thrown around like rag dolls, Clyde on the road and Bonnie in the car. Those who saw the actual ambush would say it was not far from the truth, although both were in the car. The six police officers showed no mercy for the cop-killing pair. They fired 130 rounds into the car – "We kept shooting at the car even after it stopped. We weren't taking any chances," said one of the officers.

The official report by parish coroner J. L. Wade listed 17 entrance wounds on Clyde's body and 26 on Bonnie's. Clyde's spinal column had been severed. The car was found to contain an arsenal of weapons and ammunition, and 15 sets of licence plates from various states.

News of the deaths spread like wildfire, and a crowd gathered trying to take souvenirs, including one man who attempted to cut off Clyde's trigger finger, and a woman who cut off locks of Bonnie's hair and pieces of her dress.

The funeral parlour had trouble embalming the pair, such were their injuries. Their wish to be buried together was denied by Bonnie's family, and they had separate funeral services. Even in death they remained celebrities – Bonnie's funeral attracted 20,000 people, and newspapers sold out for weeks after the ambush.

To most they were villains, to some they were heroes, but the myth has continued to grow. Were there any grounds for their actions? Are there any grounds for any murder, be the murderer male or female, be it a crime of passion, a fatal ambition, a dark secret or for revenge or retribution? Perhaps the first stanza of Bonnie Parker's poem "Suicide Sal", about a femme fatale serving time, can answer for us:

LADY KILLERS

We each of us have a good "alibi"
For being down here in the "joint"
But few of them really are justified
If you get right down to the point.

FINAL WORD

To quote the Italian poet Dante, "I had not thought death had undone so many." So many corpses, floating in rivers, curled up in barrels or burned to a cinder and swept away.

And yet this is only a small selection. The volumes that could be written about female killers would fill libraries, a rogue's gallery of women who have crossed a line that none should cross.

How many more are there; how many more will there be? As we have seen, many have lived normal lives apart from one terrible act of violence. We can never be sure if behind the next smile we meet, there's a secret that could see them behind bars, or even on death row. And for those who like to be organized, perhaps there are already notebooks filled with plans – times, dates, weapon types and alibis – just waiting to be put into action.

In reality, few women kill, but so long as there are still guns, so long as there are still knives and so long as there are still things that people can be made to ingest which could kill them, there will be murder, and not just murder committed by men. In fact, so long as there are hands to wrap around a neck, murder will be part of human life.

And there will always be new reasons to kill, and new ways of doing so. Some of these may be effective, but most will not be.

LADY KILLERS

The mistakes some of the women in this book made will be repeated. But there is always hope for a better world, and, despite the ever-present possibility of exploiting each other's mortality, perhaps some disasters – with the right guidance – can be averted.

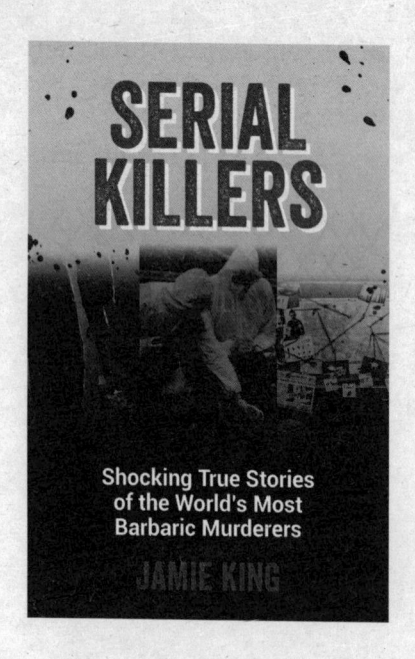

SERIAL KILLERS
Shocking True Stories of the
World's Most Barbaric Murderers

Jamie King

ISBN: 978-1-83799-122-8

A gripping compendium of some of the world's most infamous and shocking mass murderers, such as John Wayne Gacy, the Boston Strangler, the Moors murderers and Harold Shipman, as well as some lesser-known figures.

STORIES OF THE OCCULT
Supernatural Happenings and Strange Tales from Around The World

Jamie King

ISBN: 978-1-80007-934-2

Prepare to step over to the dark side with this sinister selection of occult stories. This spine-chilling compendium of strange and supernatural happenings from across the globe is essential reading, whether you're an occult enthusiast or simply curious.

Have you enjoyed this book?
If so, why not write a review on your favourite website?

If you're interested in finding out more about our books,
find us on Facebook at **Summersdale Publishers**,
on Twitter/X at **@Summersdale** and on Instagram
and TikTok at **@summersdalebooks** and get in touch.
We'd love to hear from you!

Thanks very much for buying this Summersdale book.

www.summersdale.com